Autism & PDD™ Concept Development
Food

by Pam Britton Reese and Nena C. Challenner

Skills

- concept development
- language

Ages

- 3 through 8

Grades

- PreK through 3

Evidence-Based Practice

- Early intervention that addresses skill acquisition in the areas of interaction, attention, play, comprehension, and expression will support the development of an even profile. The acquisition of key developmental skills supports the later development of communication, language, and speech and enhances emotional, social, and academic development (RCSLT, 2005).

- Many children with autism spectrum disorders learn more readily through the visual modality (RCSLT, 2005).

- Students need to understand semantic connections among words for academic success (NRP, 2000).

- Vocabulary intervention should provide opportunities for students to use target words in multiple contexts (Boone et al., 2007).

Autism & PDD Concept Development: Food incorporates these principles and is also based on expert professional practice.

References

Boone, K., Letsky, S., Wallach, S., Young, J., Gingrass, K., & Daly, C. (2007, November 28). *Role of SLP: A method of inclusion.* Paper presented at the 2007 ASHA National Convention. Retrieved March 24, 2009 from http://convention.asha.org/2007/handouts/1137_1371Letsky_Sarah__107277_Nov28_2007_Time_071812AM.ppt

National Reading Panel (NRP). (2000). *Teaching children to read: An evidence-based assessment of the scientific research literature on reading and its implications for reading instruction—Reports of the subgroups.* Retrieved March 24, 2009 from www.nichd.nih.gov/publications/nrp/upload/report.pdf

Royal College of Speech & Language Therapists (RCSLT). (2005). *Clinical guidelines for speech and language therapists.* Retrieved March 24, 2009 from www.rcslt.org/resources/clinicalguidelines

LinguiSystems

LinguiSystems, Inc.
3100 4th Avenue
East Moline, IL 61244
800-776-4332

FAX: 800-577-4555
Email: service@linguisystems.com
Web: linguisystems.com

Copyright © 2001 LinguiSystems, Inc.

All of our products are copyrighted to protect the fine work of our authors. You may only copy the student materials as needed for your own use. Any other reproduction or distribution of the pages in this book is prohibited, including copying the entire book to use as another primary source or "master" copy.

Printed in the U.S.A.

ISBN 10: 0-7606-0389-8
ISBN 13: 978-0-7606-0389-5

About the Authors

Pam Britton Reese, M.A., CCC-SLP, owns a private practice, CommunicAid Plus, where she provides speech and language services to children and adults. She is also an educational consultant to public and private schools. Pam has over nine years experience in the schools as a speech-language pathologist and teacher of the hearing-impaired. She has worked with children with autism and PDD since 1995. *Autism & PDD: Concept Development* is her fourth publication with LinguiSystems.

Nena C. Challenner, M.Ed., is a Community-Based Instruction Teacher and Inclusion Specialist. She has been a teacher for over 15 years and has taught preschool through second grade. She has worked with children with autism and PDD since 1995. Nena is also a reading consultant at CommunicAid Plus. *Autism & PDD: Concept Development* is her third publication with LinguiSystems.

Dedication

For the children at CommunicAid Plus (CAP Kids!)

Edited by Lauri Whiskeyman
Illustrations by Margaret Warner
Page Layout by Christine Buysse

Table of Contents

Introduction 5

    Water 9

    Milk 21

    Sandwich 33

    Ice Cream 45

    Apple 57

    Banana 69

    Carrot 81

    Corn 93

    Hamburger 105

    Bread 117

Extension Activities 129

Suggested Literature 143

Picture Communication Symbols (PCS) © 1981-2000.
Reprinted with the permission of Mayer-Johnson, Inc., P.O. Box 1579,
Solana Beach, CA 92075-7579, 1-800-588-4548, *www.mayer-johnson.com*

Burger King	page 110
go	page 13
into/in	page 24
McDonald's	page 110
middle	pages 38, 39, 40, and 109

Introduction

In our work with children with autism, we were often surprised at misconceptions our students had about the world. For example, when 9-year-old Katie was asked, "What would you do if you saw a house on fire?" she answered, "Roast marshmallows." She had only experienced fire in this way and was unable to perceive that fire might also be dangerous, that it burns, or that it can heat a home. Other children with autism whom we have known didn't recognize a sitting dog as a dog or a rocking chair as a chair. These are concepts that typically-developing children are able to process through observing or listening to information and instantly linking to other learned concepts. We know that children with autism must be taught such language skills as naming attributes, placing words in appropriate categories, and giving descriptions.

It is well documented that children with autism learn more easily when information is presented in a visual format. The picture is constant and the child can view it until the concept is learned, as opposed to the transient nature of speech. Most books published for young children, however, do not teach the concepts the child with autism needs to learn. Although the stories are often engaging and the artwork of museum quality, they too often confuse the child with autism. Foxes that drive? Animals that wear clothing and talk? Cars with eyes? Although amusing, they are not a realistic depiction of our world. Often, too, the art is very complex with many extraneous details. (A list of some books we found that did a good job of teaching concepts is included on page 143.)

Each book in *Autism & PDD: Concept Development* covers 10 concepts around a theme:

- Animals
- Clothing
- Food
- Household Items
- Toys and Entertainment
- Transportation

Specific attributes and features of each concept are illustrated with large pictures, simple sentences, and picture symbols. In addition, there are questions to check comprehension and activities to help the child apply this knowledge to other contexts. These books were developed for professionals who work with children with autism, ages 3 through 8. However, these books can also be used with children who have language delays or language disorders caused by disabilities such as Down syndrome. Parents and caregivers can also use these stories and activities.

How to Use this Book

This book contains concepts about 10 different foods. Each concept is illustrated in both a large-page and mini-page format for making books to read to the child. We suggest that the large-page format be copied. Place the pages in plastic page protectors. Sliding a thin piece of cardboard or card stock into the pocket between the pages will stiffen the pages and make

Introduction, continued

them easier for young children to turn. Put the pages into folders with brads or three-ring notebooks to create a book. You may want to put a copy of the first page of each unit on the front of the folder or notebook. The mini-pages can be made into small books for the children to take home after they've heard the story at school.

You may want to use all of the concepts in the book at one time to introduce or extend a thematic unit or you can select a specific concept to focus on. For example, a child might know dog and cat, but have no idea what a rabbit is! Remember to go at the child's pace. A child might need many lessons on chairs, for example, before moving on to other concepts in the book.

Comprehension Questions

A variety of comprehension questions (e.g., *yes-no, wh-, how*) follow each concept. The questions can be used in different ways. Some children may only be able to answer the *yes-no* questions. Some children may do better with the *wh-* and *how* questions. You can ask the questions after each concept is taught or after each page. If a child has difficulty answering a question, go through the targeted concept again and help him or her find the answer. Cue the child by pointing to the picture and/or text as you ask the question again.

Generalization Pages

Each concept has a generalization exercise. This exercise is designed to check the child's comprehension of the concept as well as to extend understanding of the concept to different forms and views. Many of the children we work with understand only one form of a concept: "That is a cat. That cat is gray. Thus, all cats must be gray or they are not cats." As you can see, that is a false generalization. By presenting variations of the same concept such as size, color, and position, the child learns to expand his or her mental definition of the concept.

After you read about the targeted concept, make a copy of the generalization page for the child. Read the directions aloud and have the child complete the page. Then encourage the child to describe the circled concepts. Depending on the child's level, the responses could be as simple as labeling "shirt" or as elaborate as "The shirt has long sleeves." You can also use the pictures on this page to point out the differences between the circled concepts.

Extension Activities

The activities suggested at the end of the book give the child the opportunity to experience the new concepts in a natural setting. Although children with autism learn concepts more easily in a visual format that never changes (e.g., the stories), it is equally important to give the child the opportunity to taste that apple or see the balloon fly around the room. Each activity page contains a list of materials needed to complete the activity, instructions for the adult, and Picture Prompt Cards. The Picture Prompt Cards may be used in a variety of ways. Some suggestions are:

Introduction, *continued*

1. Copy the cards and glue them onto index cards or put them on a communication board. Use them to prompt the appropriate behaviors in each activity.

2. Make two copies of each card and use for a matching game.

3. Copy the cards to send home for families to repeat the activities at home.

Suggested Literature

We have included a list of children's literature to help extend and promote generalization of the concepts to other contexts. These books were carefully chosen because of their simple text and realistic pictures. It is important to provide as many opportunities as possible for the child with autism to see and hear the concept. We have found that repeated exposure to the concepts in *Autism & PDD: Concept Development*, followed by other books with different pictures and texts, aids the child with autism in generalizing the concept to different contexts.

Closing

Remember that the concepts covered in the book can be taught in classrooms as well as group or individual therapy sessions. We hope that the children you work with enjoy the books as much as our students and clients do.

Pam and Nena

Note: Some children may have food allergies.
Make food substitutions as needed.

Water

I drink water.

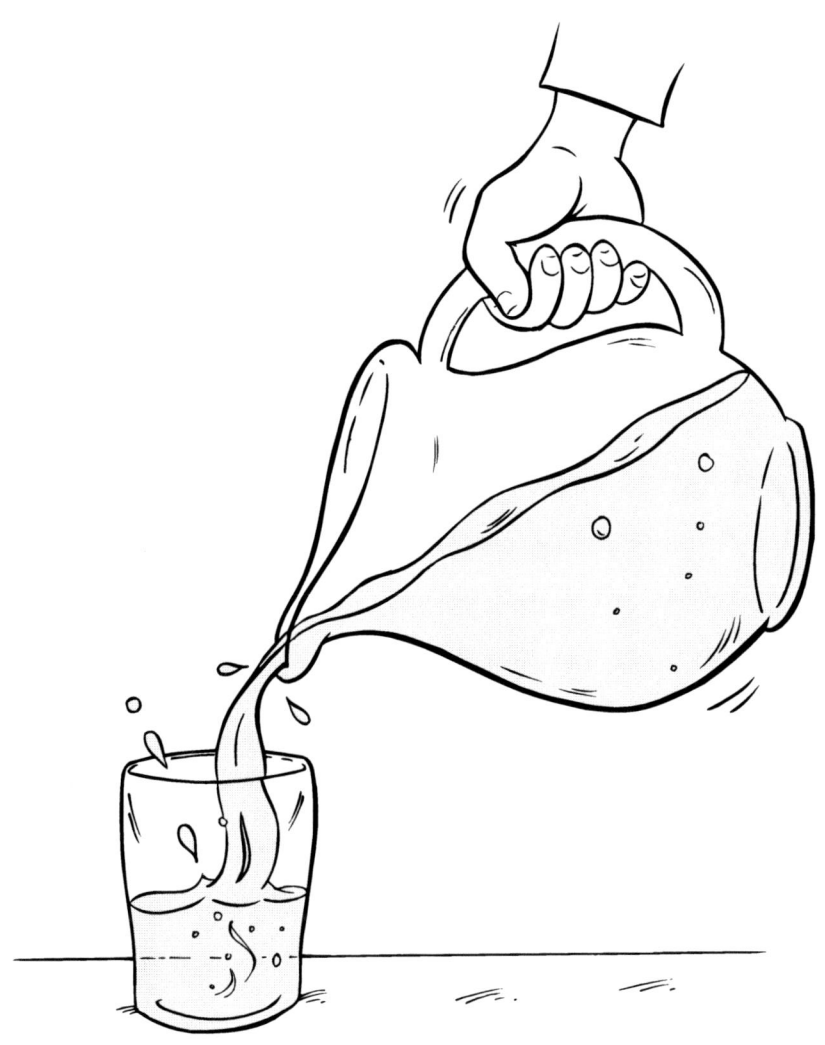

 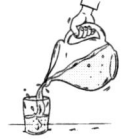 

I pour water into a cup or glass.

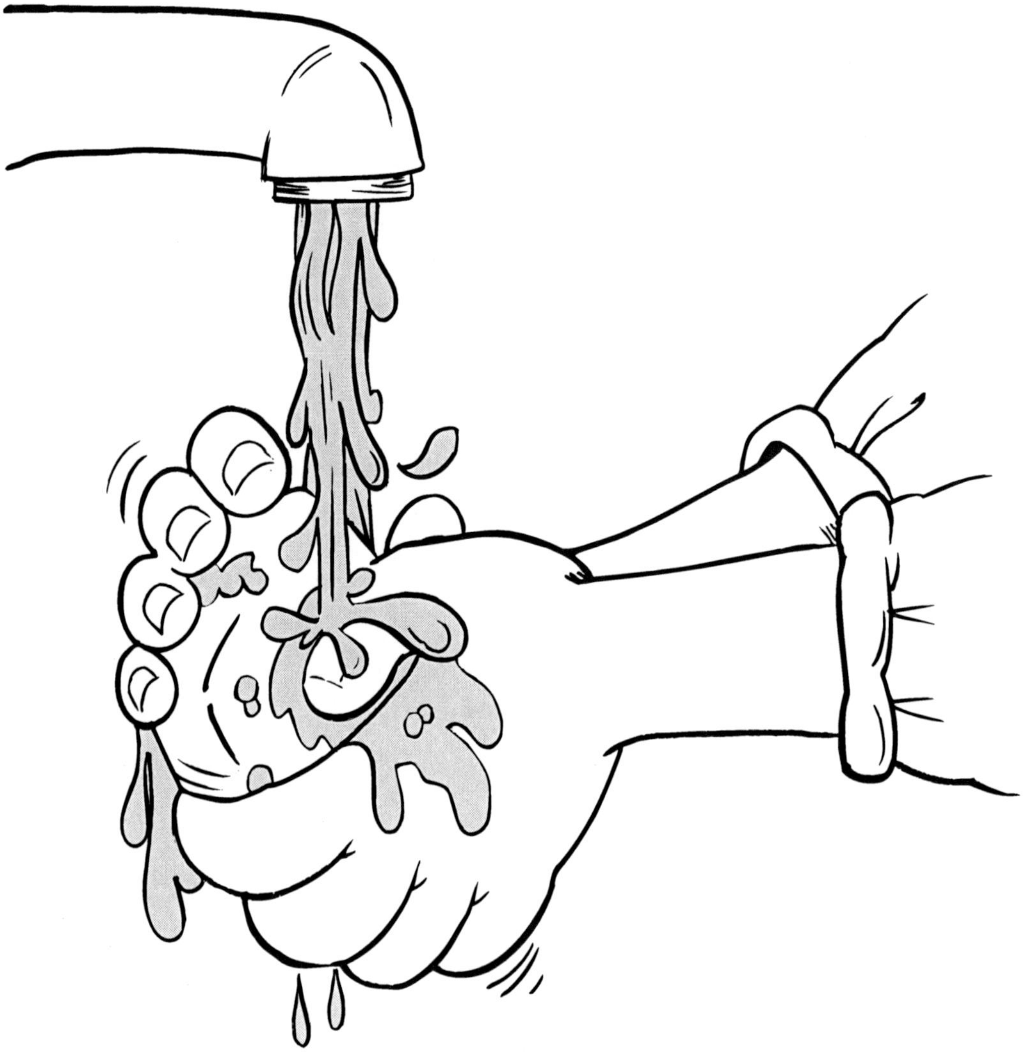

I wash my hands in water.

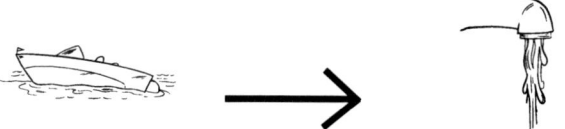

A boat goes in water.

I swim in water.

Flowers need water.

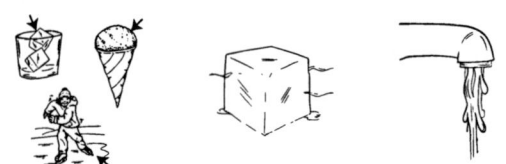

Ice is frozen water.

Rain is water.

Concept: Water

Yes-No Questions

1. Is ice water?
2. Is milk water?
3. Do you sleep in water?
4. Do you drink water?
5. Do you pour water in a hat?
6. Does a bicycle go in water?
7. Do flowers need water?
8. Do you wash your hands in water?
9. Does rain come from clouds?
10. Does water make you wet?

Wh- and How Questions

1. Where do you swim?
2. How do you wash your hands?
3. Who drinks water?
4. When do you drink water?
5. Where do you pour water?
6. Where does a boat go?
7. What is ice?
8. What do flowers need?
9. Where does rain come from?
10. What makes you wet?

Water Generalization Page

Circle the water. Put an X on each picture that is not water.

Water Mini-Book

Copy this page. Cut apart the boxes on the dotted lines. Put the story in order to make a little book and staple.

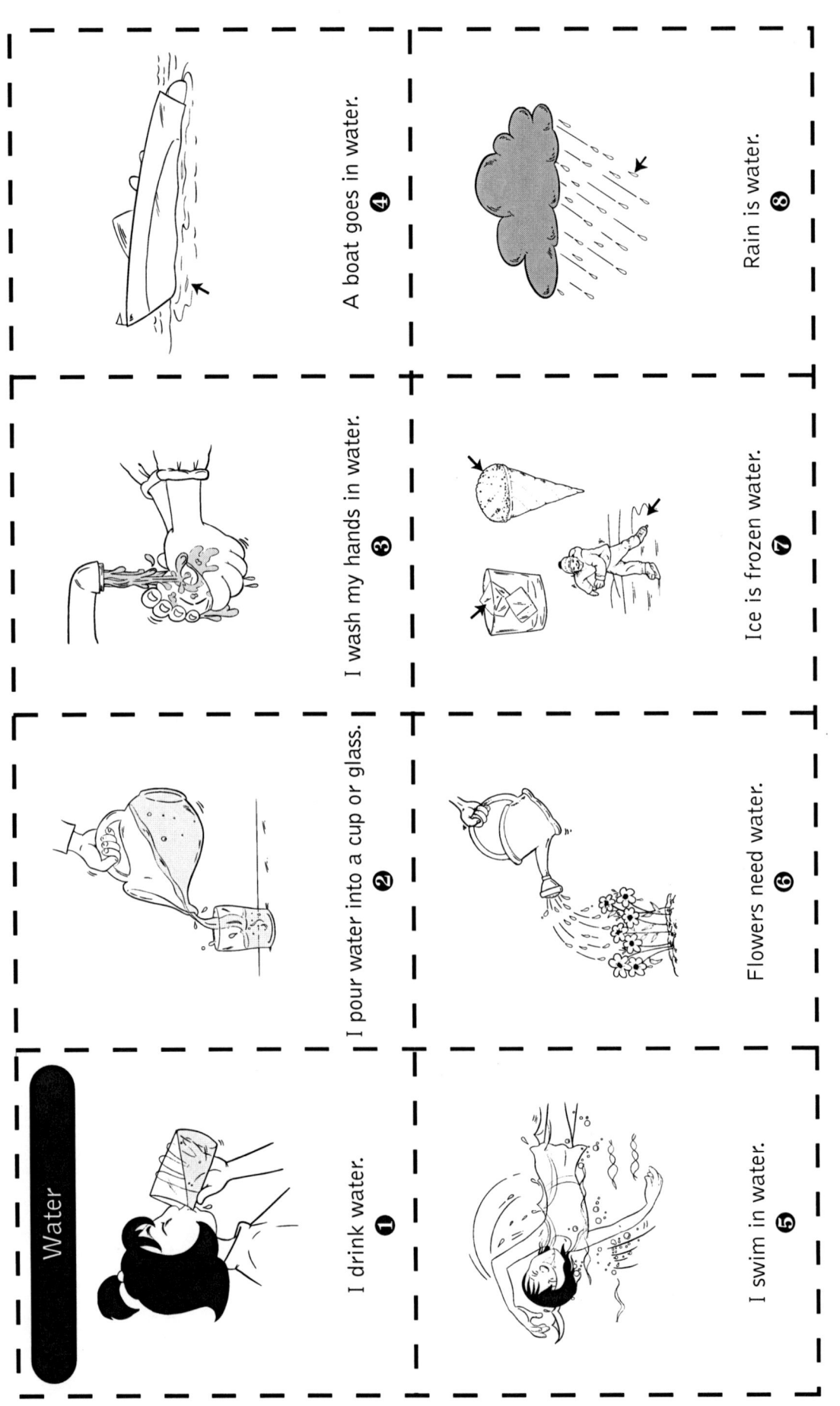

Milk

Milk is a white drink.

I drink milk.

I pour milk into a cup or glass.

Cows make milk.

We buy milk at the grocery store.

Milk goes in the refrigerator.

Milk is in ice cream and cheese.

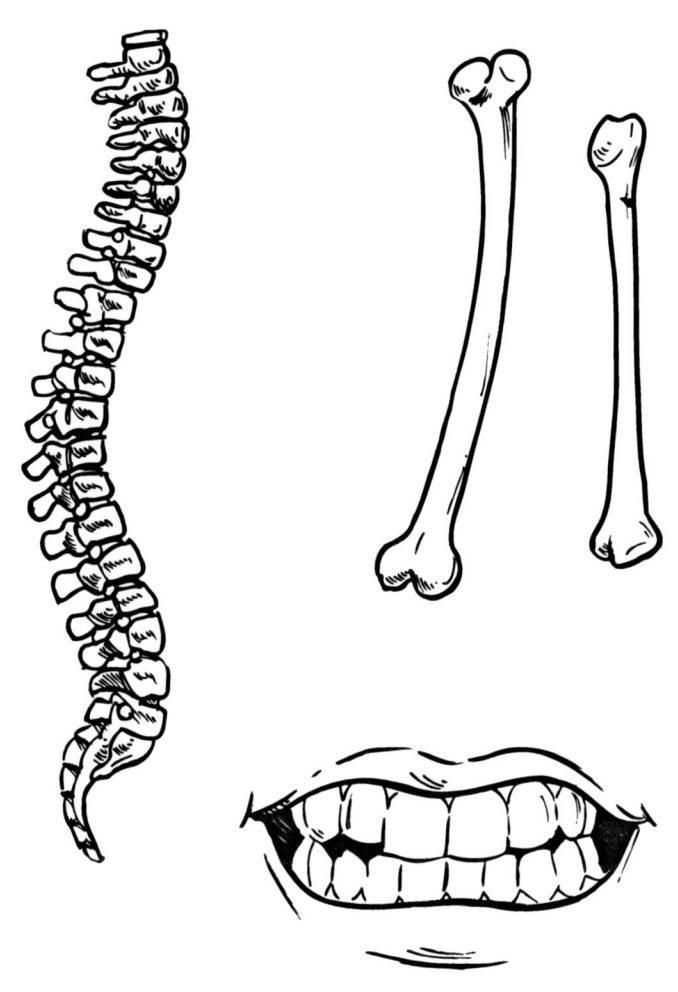

 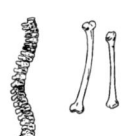  

Milk makes my bones and teeth strong.

Concept: Milk

Yes-No Questions

1. Is milk a drink?
2. Do birds make milk?
3. Do you buy milk at the grocery store?
4. Does milk stay in the oven?
5. Is milk in eggs?
6. Does milk make bones strong?
7. Is milk in ice cream?
8. Is milk green?
9. Can you pour milk?
10. Do you drink milk from a plate?

Wh- and How Questions

1. What color is milk?
2. Who drinks milk?
3. Where can you buy milk?
4. Which animal makes milk?
5. Where can you pour milk?
6. What is ice cream made with?
7. Where does milk stay cold?
8. What is cheese made with?
9. How does milk help your bones and teeth?
10. What do you like to drink?

Milk Generalization Page

Circle the milk. Put an X on each picture that is not milk.

Milk
Concept Development

Milk Mini-Book

Copy this page. Cut apart the boxes on the dotted lines. Put the story in order to make a little book and staple.

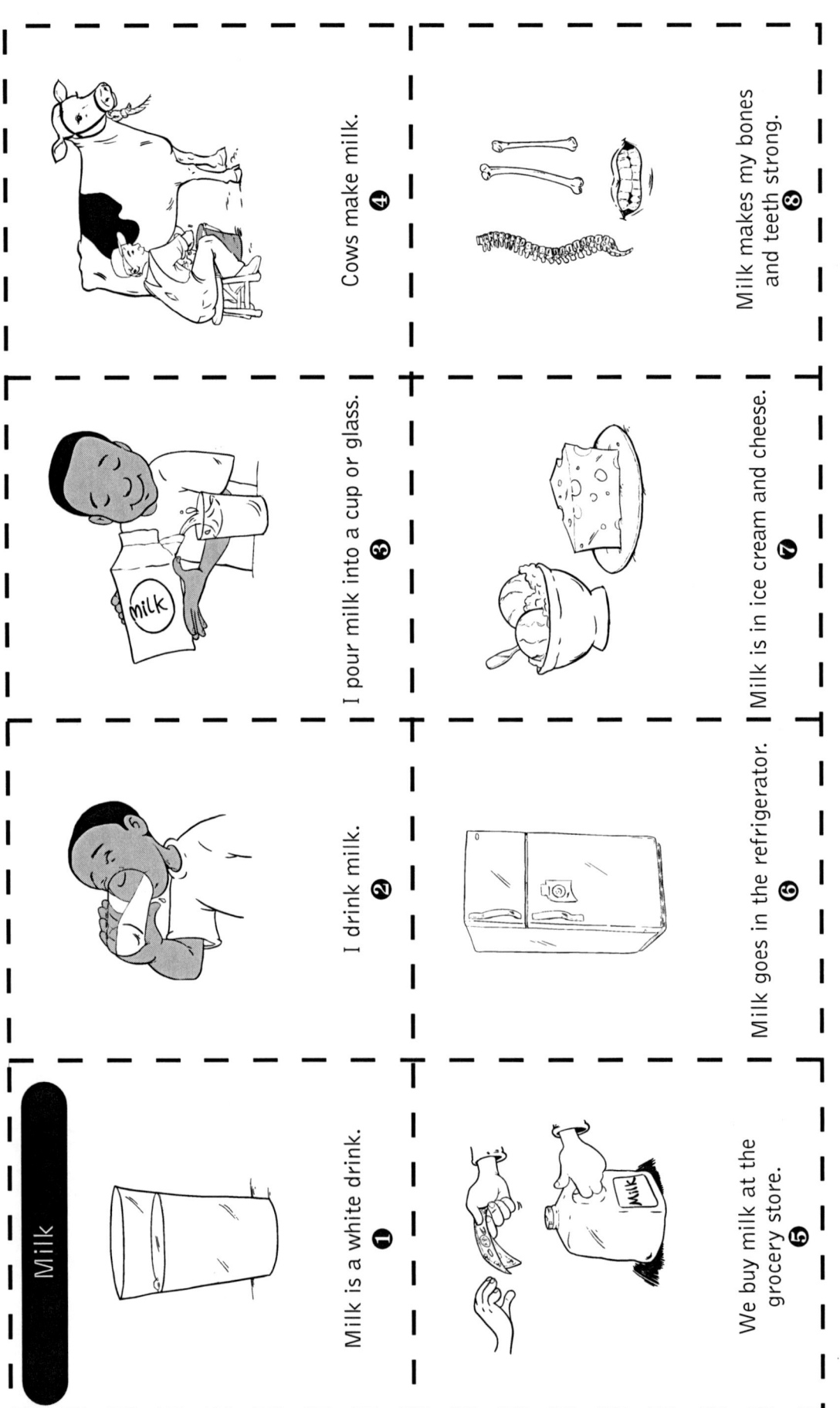

Milk
Concept Development

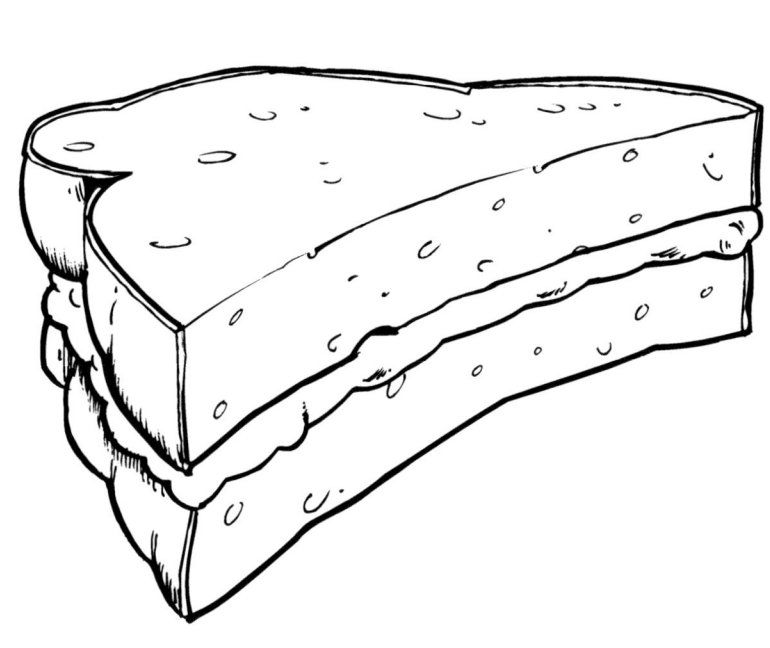

Sandwich

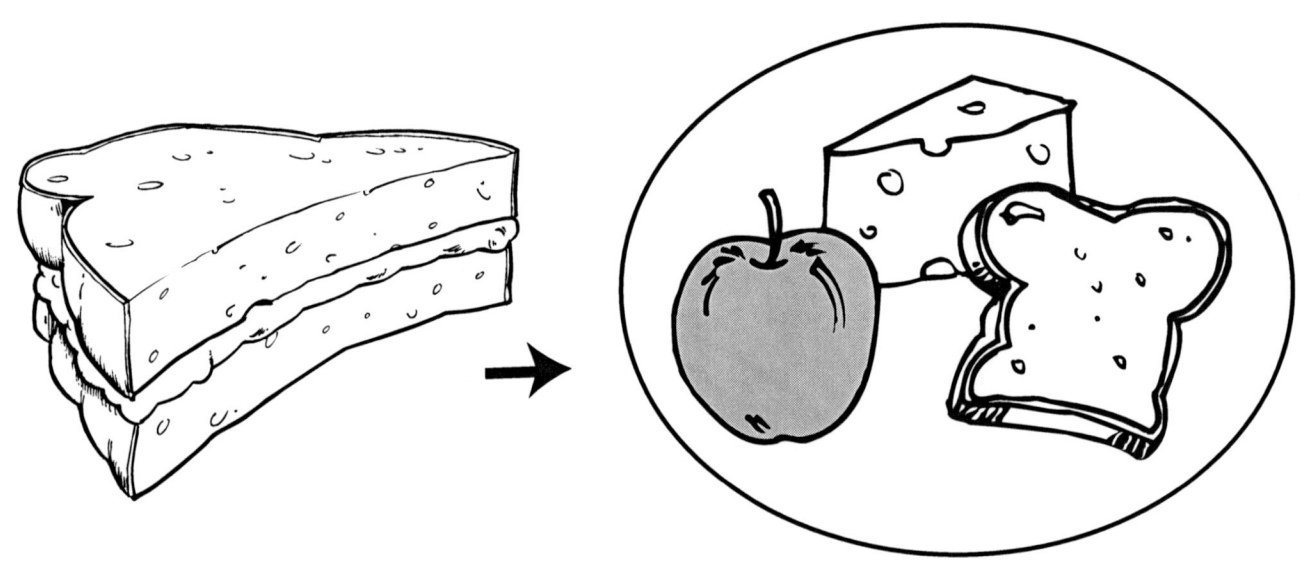

A sandwich is food.

I can eat a sandwich.

I can eat a sandwich for lunch.

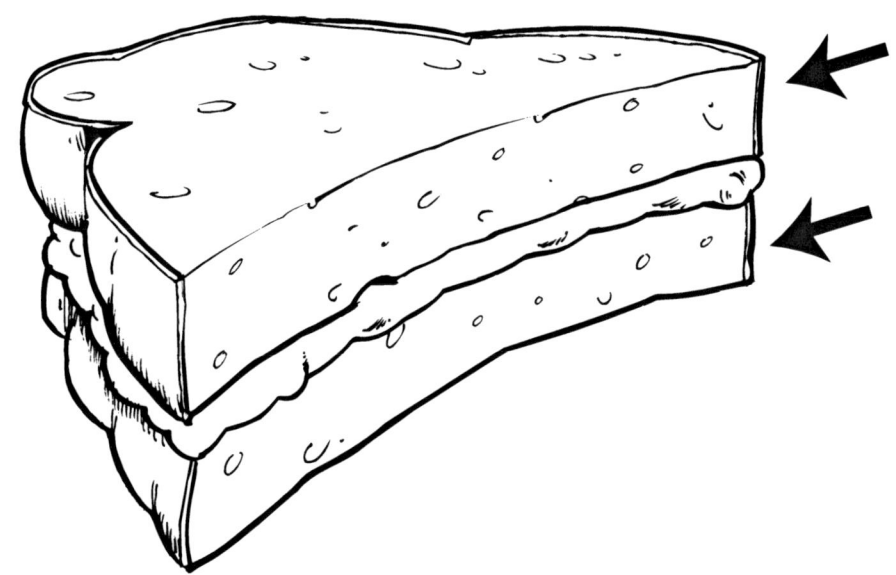

 **2**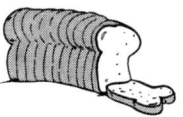

A sandwich has two pieces of bread.

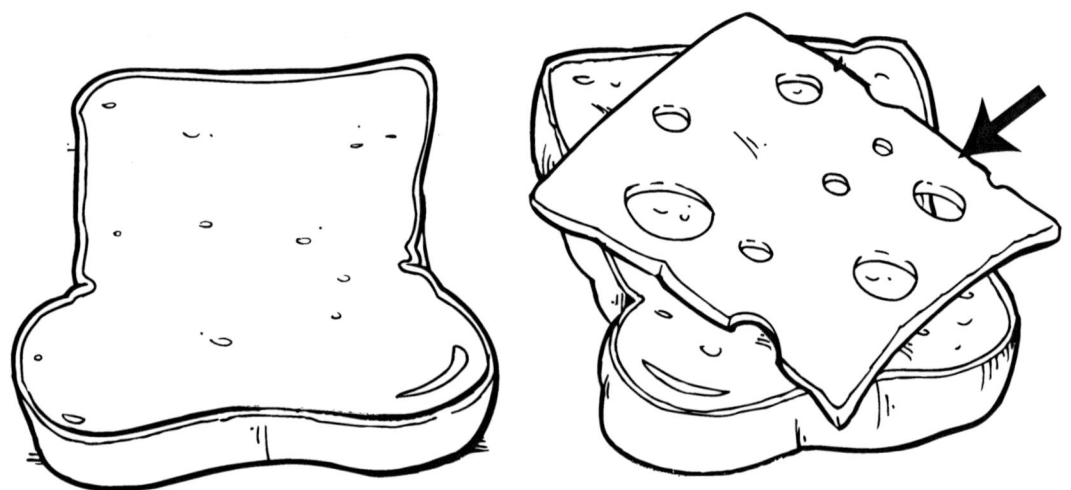

A cheese sandwich has cheese in the middle.

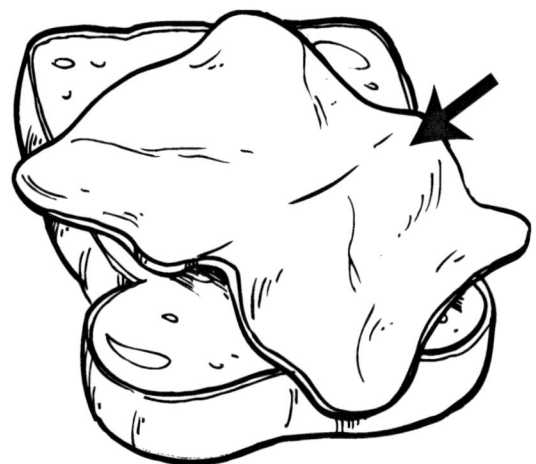

A ham sandwich has ham in the middle.

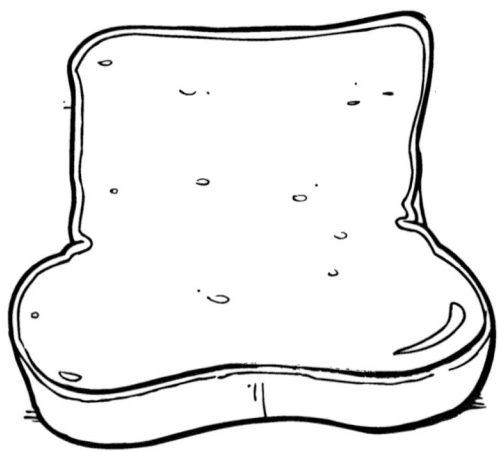
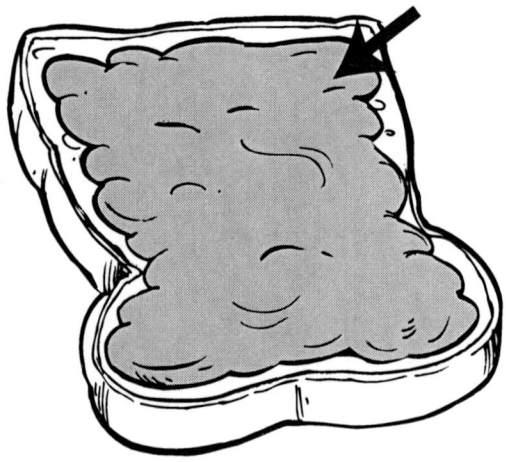

 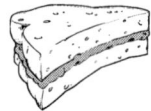 

A peanut butter sandwich has peanut butter in the middle.

I can eat a sandwich with my hands.

Concept: Sandwich

Yes-No Questions

1. Is a sandwich food?
2. Is a sandwich a toy?
3. Can you drink a sandwich?
4. Can you eat a sandwich for lunch?
5. Does a sandwich have two slices of bread?
6. Is cheese in the middle of a peanut butter sandwich?
7. Is peanut butter in the middle of a peanut butter sandwich?
8. Do you eat a sandwich with a spoon?
9. Can ham be in the middle of a sandwich?
10. Does a sandwich have two slices of cake?

Wh- and How Questions

1. What can you do with a sandwich?
2. When can you eat a sandwich?
3. How many slices of bread make a sandwich?
4. Who eats a sandwich?
5. Where is the cheese in a cheese sandwich?
6. How do we eat sandwiches?
7. What is in the middle of a peanut butter sandwich?
8. How do you make a ham sandwich?
9. What can you eat for lunch?
10. What is your favorite sandwich?

Sandwich Generalization Page

Circle the sandwiches. Put an X on each picture that is not a sandwich.

Sandwich Mini-Book

Copy this page. Cut apart the boxes on the dotted lines. Put the story in order to make a little book and staple.

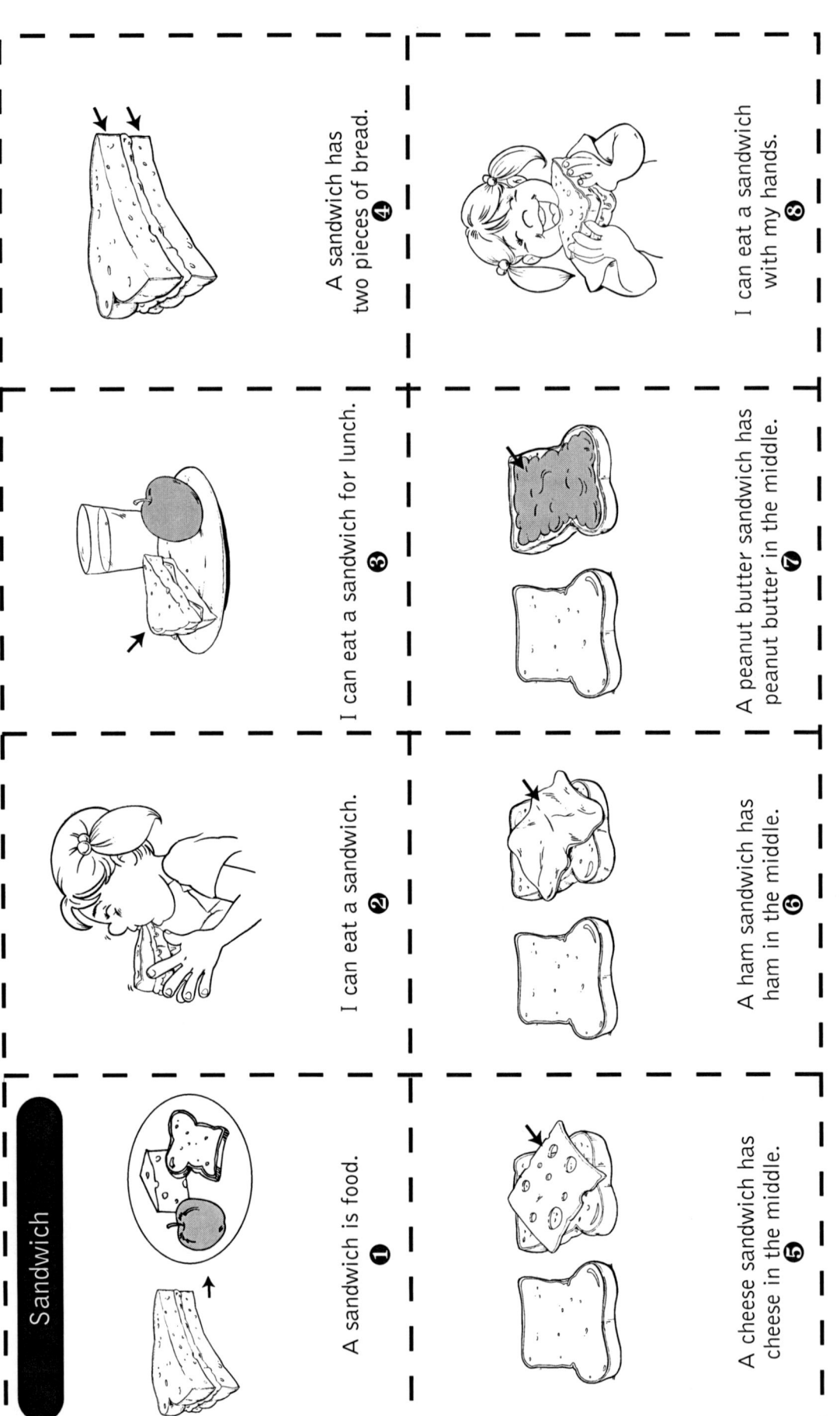

Sandwich

A sandwich is food. ①

I can eat a sandwich. ②

I can eat a sandwich for lunch. ③

A sandwich has two pieces of bread. ④

A cheese sandwich has cheese in the middle. ⑤

A ham sandwich has ham in the middle. ⑥

A peanut butter sandwich has peanut butter in the middle. ⑦

I can eat a sandwich with my hands. ⑧

Sandwich
Concept Development

Copyright © 2001 LinguiSystems, Inc.

Ice cream is food.

Ice cream is sweet.

Ice cream may be chocolate or vanilla.

Ice cream is cold.

 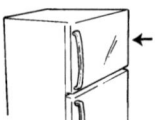

Ice cream stays in the freezer.

Ice cream melts.

I can eat ice cream in a bowl with a spoon.

I can lick ice cream on a cone.

Concept: Ice Cream

Yes-No Questions

1. Is ice cream a toy?
2. Is ice cream cold?
3. Does ice cream taste sweet?
4. Can you have green bean ice cream?
5. Does ice cream stay in the drawer?
6. Do you eat ice cream with a knife?
7. Do you like chocolate ice cream?
8. Does ice cream melt?
9. Is all ice cream vanilla?
10. Is ice cream a food?

Wh- and How Questions

1. How does ice cream taste?
2. Where do you keep ice cream?
3. How do you eat an ice-cream cone?
4. What is one flavor of ice cream?
5. How do you eat ice cream in a bowl?
6. Why does ice cream stay in the freezer?
7. What is a cold food?
8. What food tastes sweet?
9. What melts?
10. What is your favorite ice cream?

Ice Cream Generalization Page

Circle the ice cream. Put an X on each picture that is not ice cream.

Ice Cream Mini-Book

Copy this page. Cut apart the boxes on the dotted lines. Put the story in order to make a little book and staple.

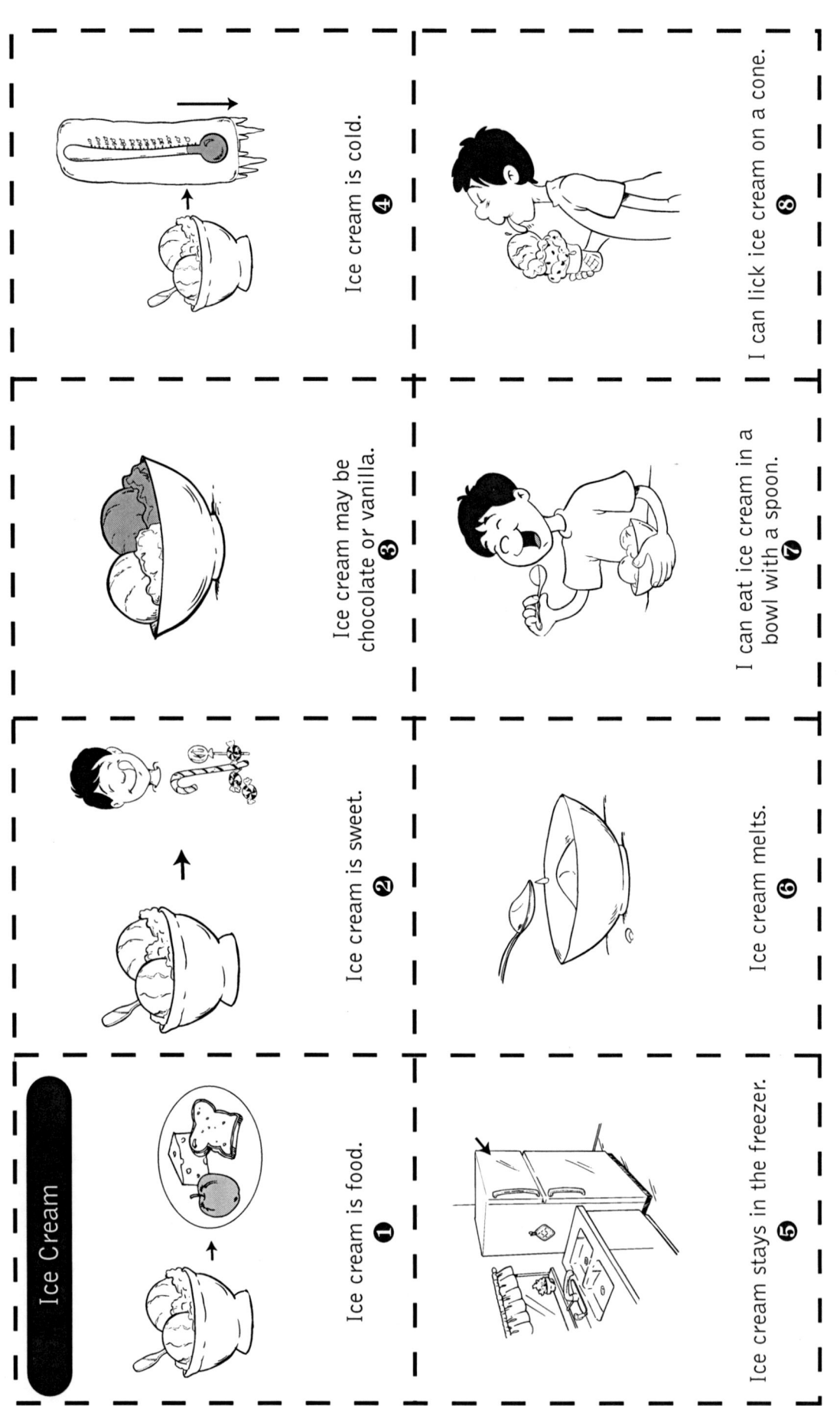

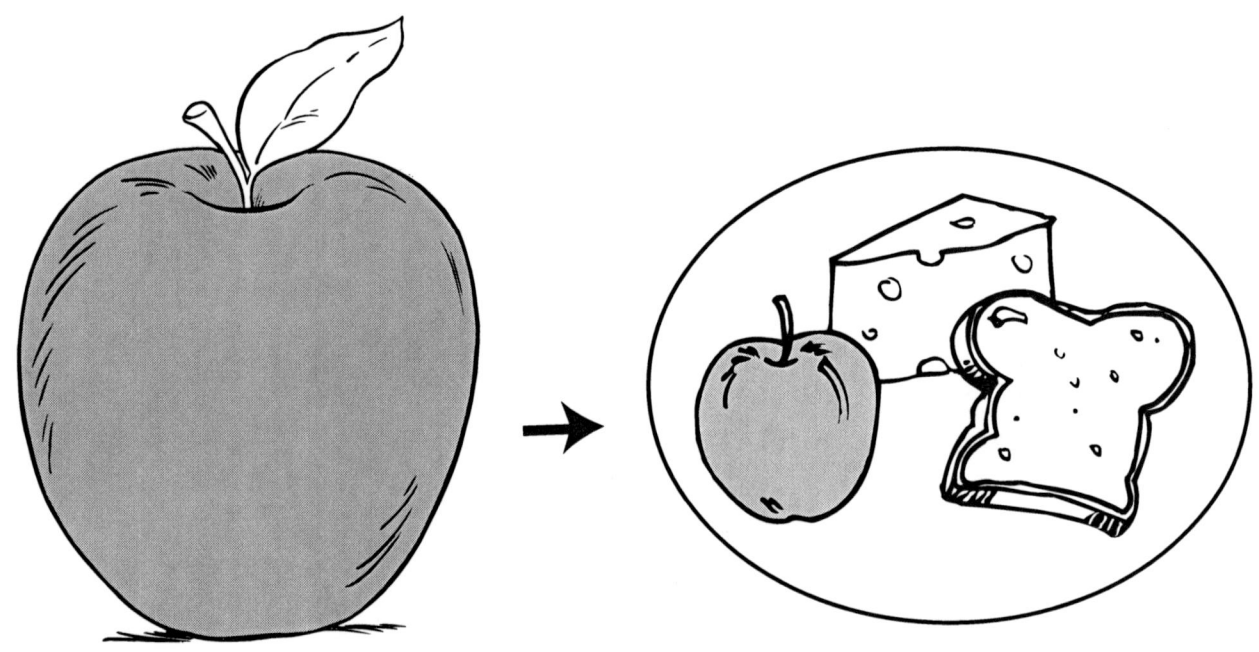

An apple is food.

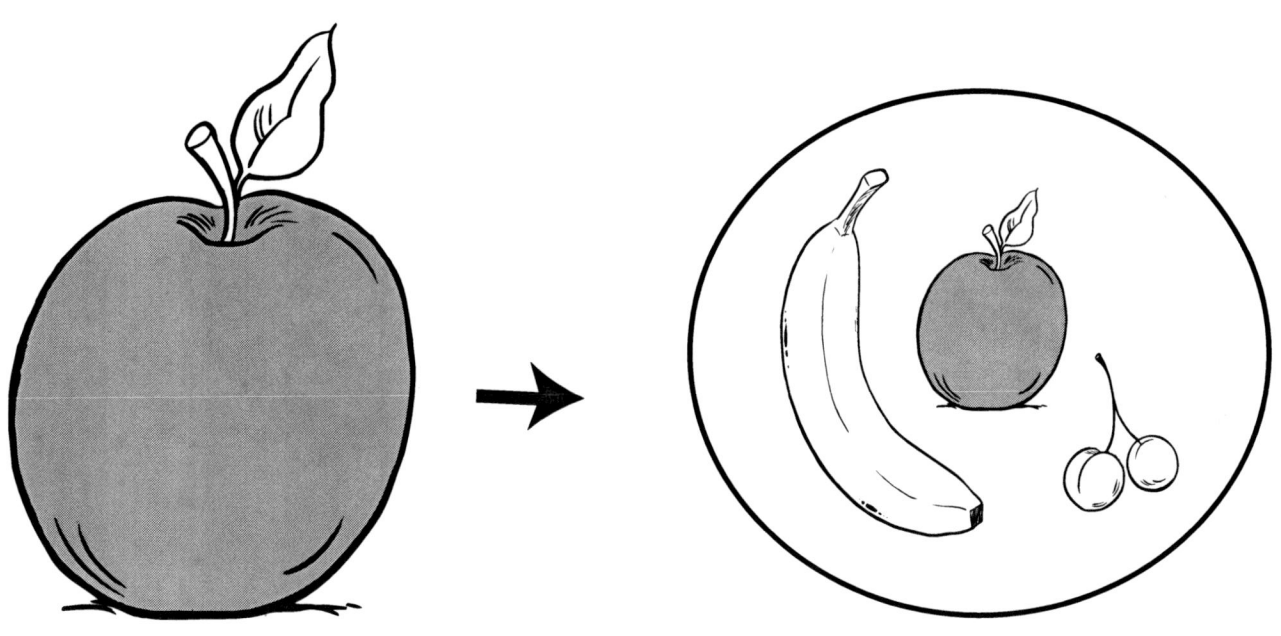

An apple is a fruit.

Apples grow on trees.

Apples are red, yellow, or green.

I can eat an apple with my hands.

Apples are crunchy.

Apples are in apple juice.

Apples are in applesauce.

Concept: Apple

Yes-No Questions

1. Is an apple food?
2. Is an apple a meat?
3. Do apples grow on the ground?
4. Are apples red?
5. Are apples blue?
6. Can you eat an apple with your hands?
7. Are apples soft?
8. Are apples in apple juice?
9. Are apples in applesauce?
10. Do you like apple juice?

Wh- and How Questions

1. Where do apples grow?
2. What color are apples?
3. How do you eat apples?
4. Who eats applesauce?
5. What fruit is crunchy?
6. Which juice do apples make?
7. What is an apple?
8. What grows on apple trees?
9. What can you make with apples?
10. What fruit do you like to eat?

Apple Generalization Page

Circle the apples. Put an X on each picture that does not show an apple.

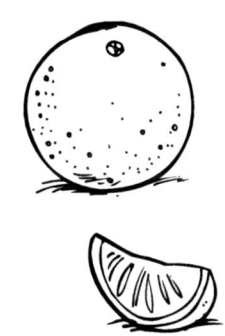

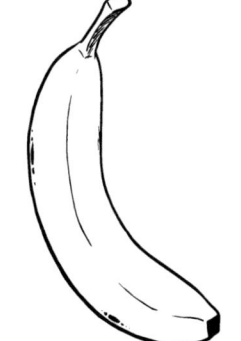

Apple Mini-Book

Copy this page. Cut apart the boxes on the dotted lines. Put the story in order to make a little book and staple.

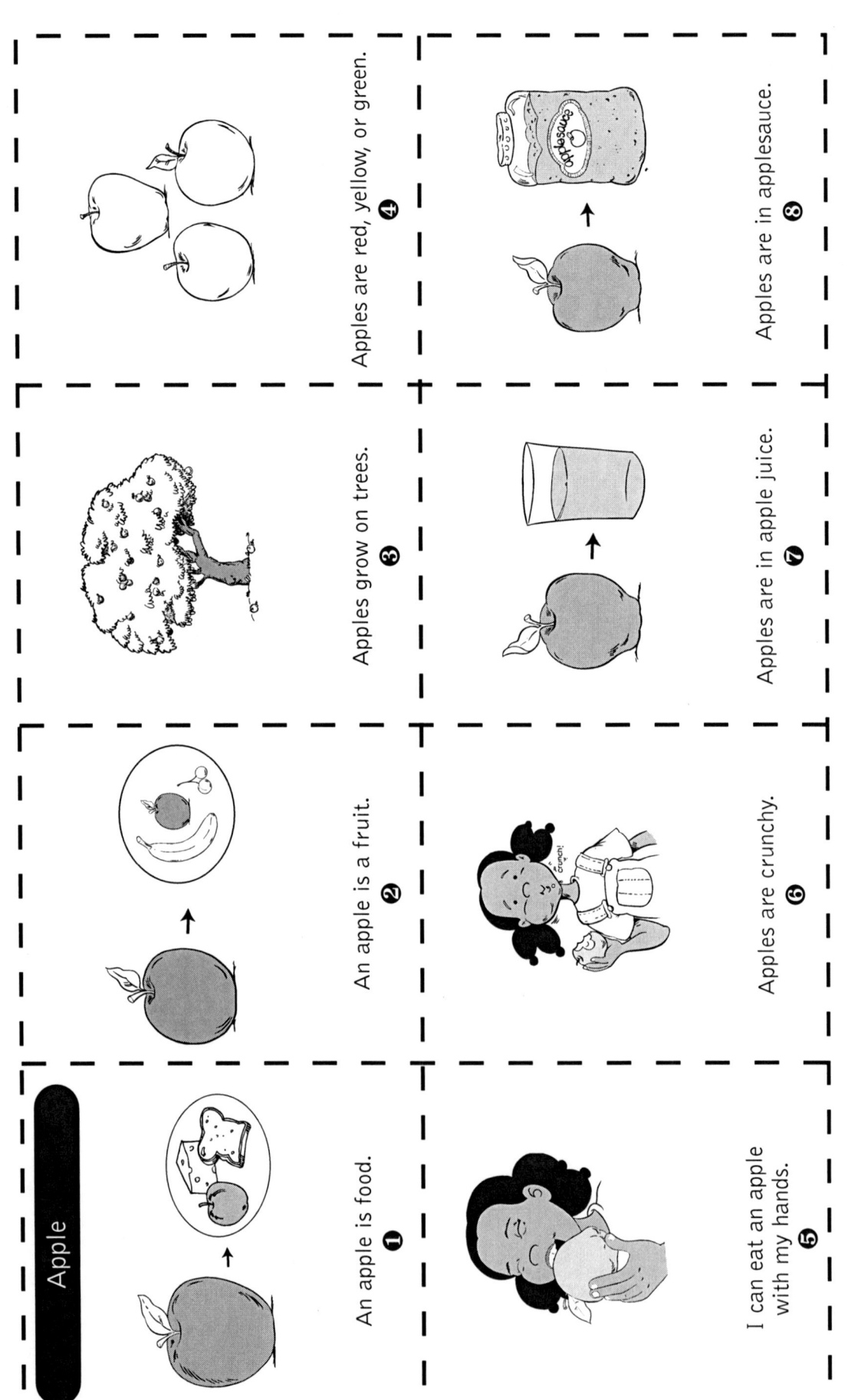

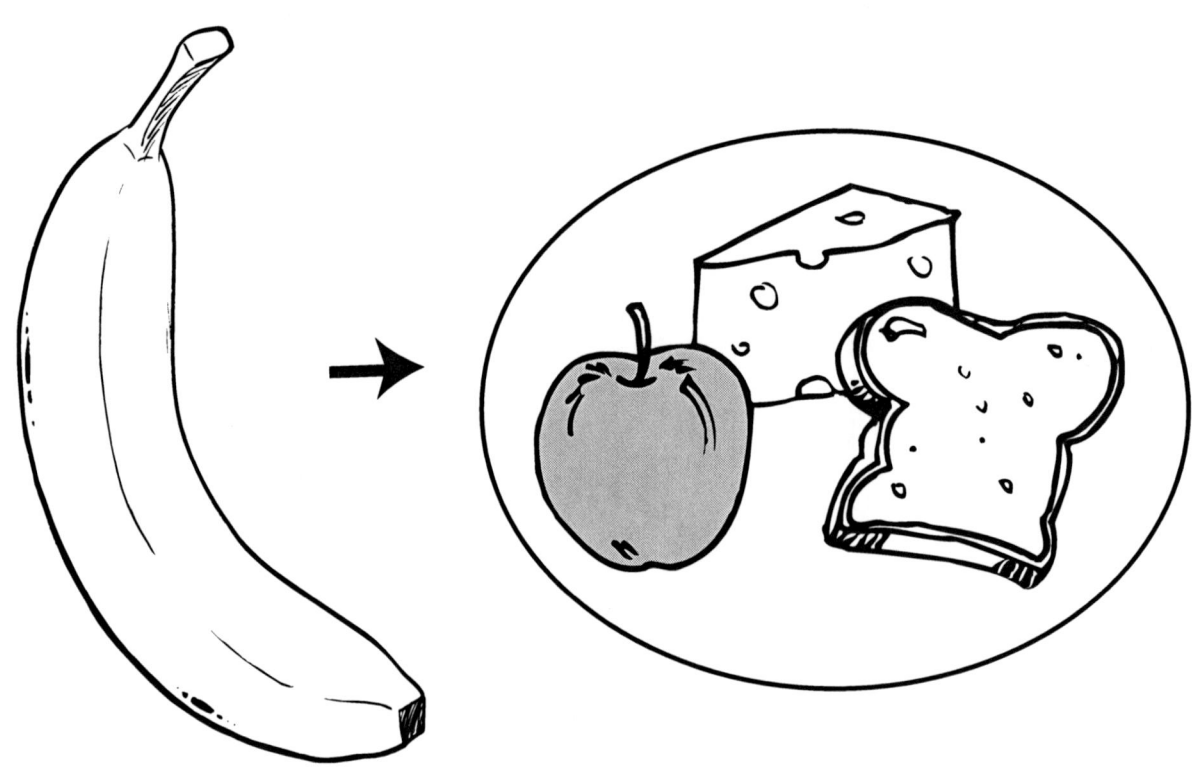

A banana is food.

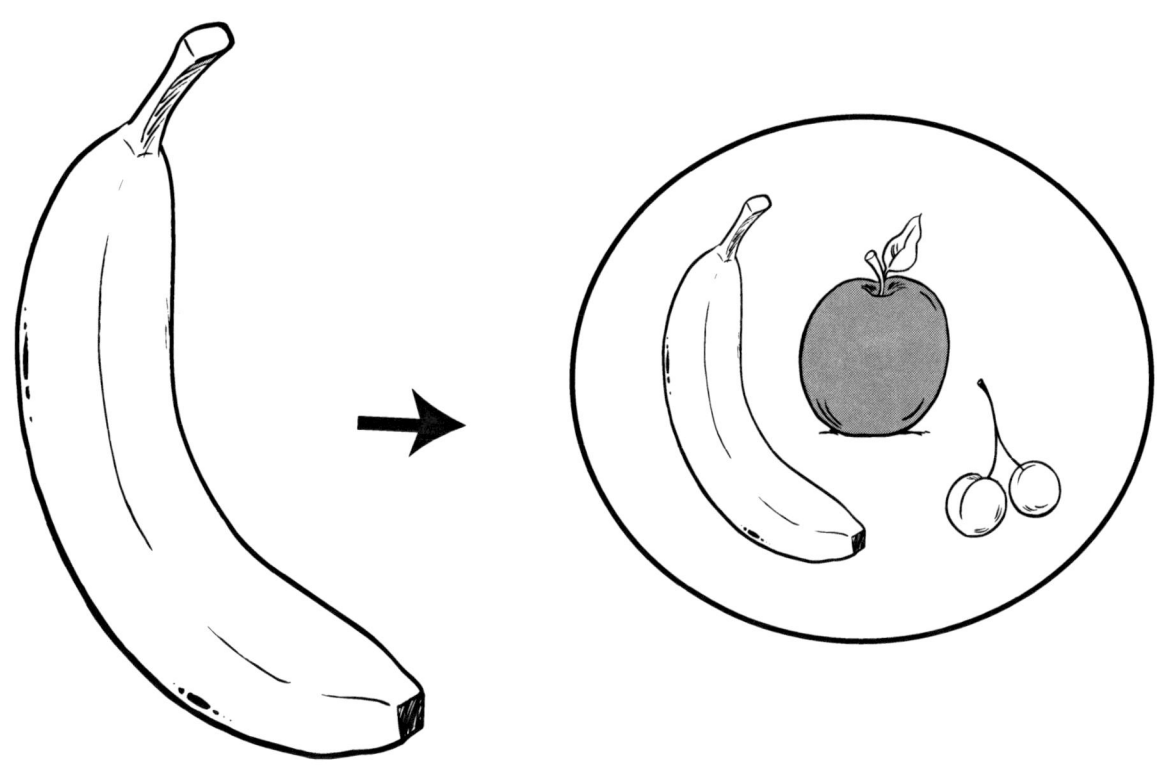

A banana is a fruit.

Bananas grow on large plants.

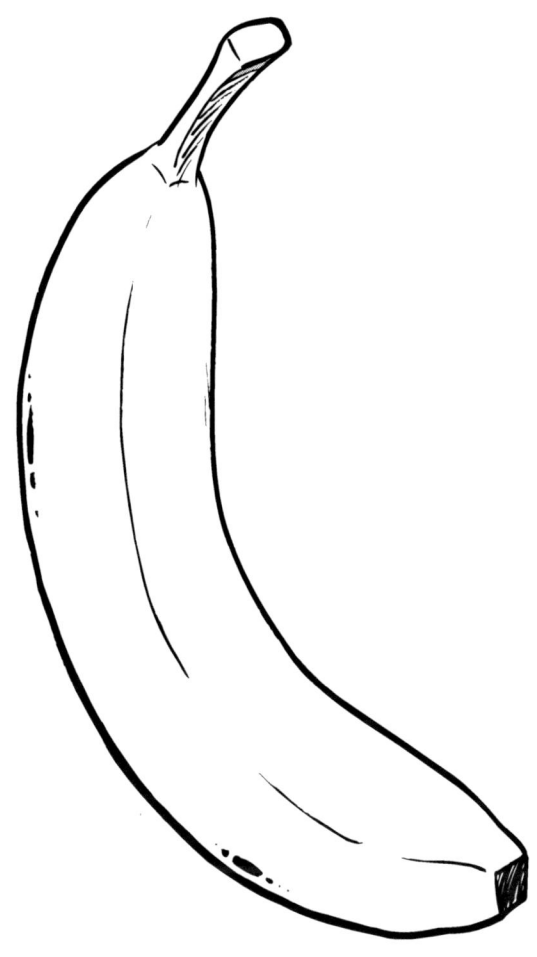

Bananas are yellow.

I peel a banana.

I can eat a banana with my hands.

Bananas are soft when I bite them.

Monkeys like bananas too.

Concept: Banana

Yes-No Questions

1. Is a banana a candy?
2. Is a banana a fruit?
3. Do bananas grow under the ground?
4. Is a banana peel red?
5. Is a banana peel yellow?
6. Do you peel a banana before you eat it?
7. Is a banana crunchy?
8. Is a banana soft?
9. Do monkeys like to eat bananas?
10. Do you like to eat bananas?

Wh- and How Questions

1. Where do bananas grow?
2. What color are banana peels?
3. How do you eat bananas?
4. When can you eat a banana?
5. Who eats bananas?
6. Which animal likes bananas?
7. What is a banana?
8. What fruit is soft to eat?
9. What is a banana: a food or an animal?
10. What fruit do you like to eat?

Banana Generalization Page

Circle the bananas. Put an X on each picture that does not show a banana.

Banana Mini-Book

Copy this page. Cut apart the boxes on the dotted lines. Put the story in order to make a little book and staple.

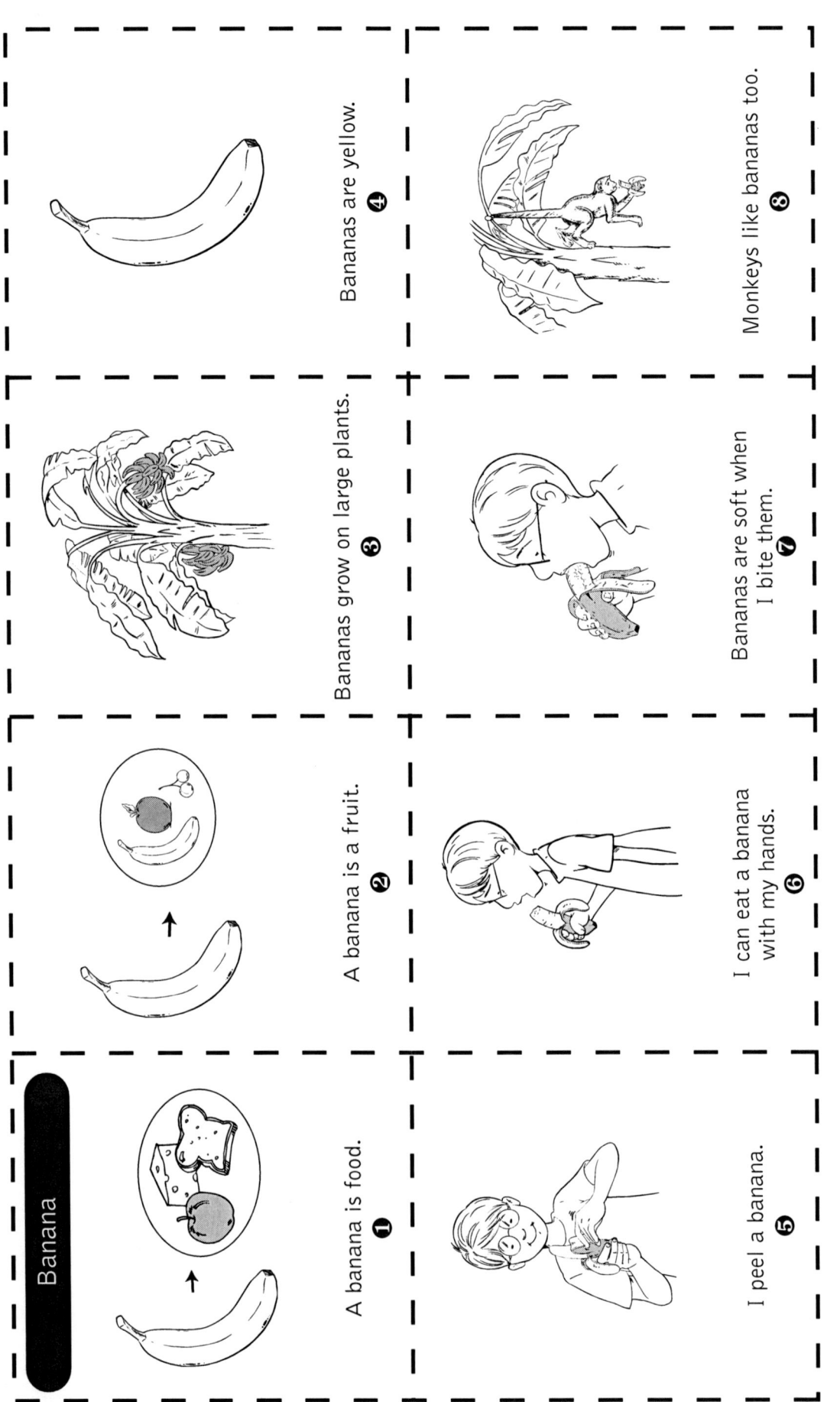

Carrot

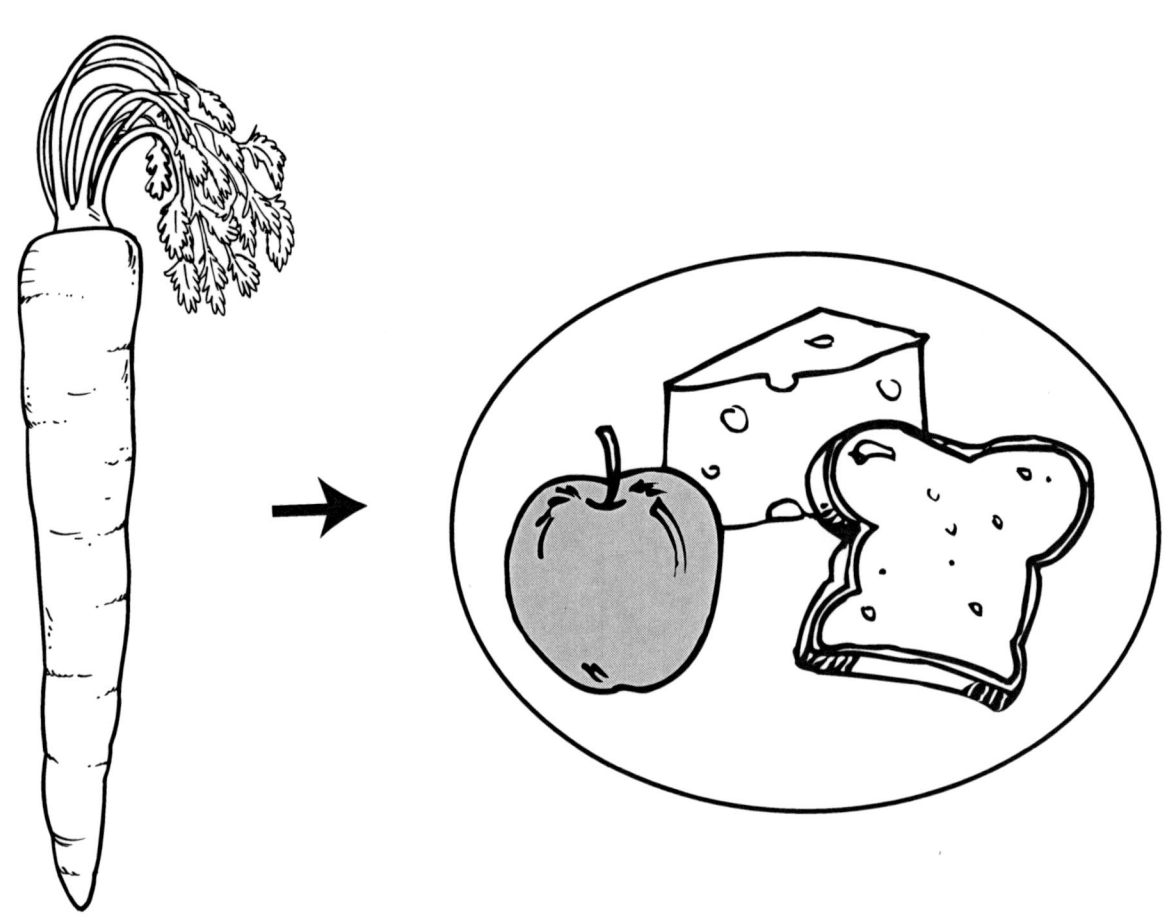

A carrot is food.

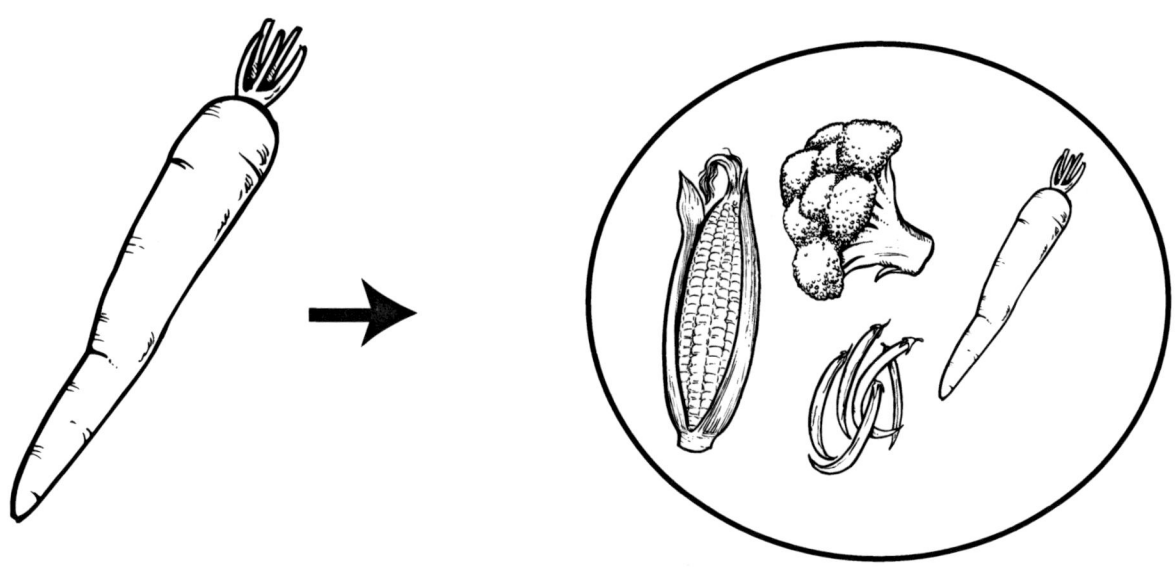

A carrot is a vegetable.

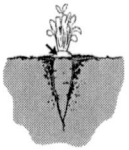

Carrots grow under the ground.

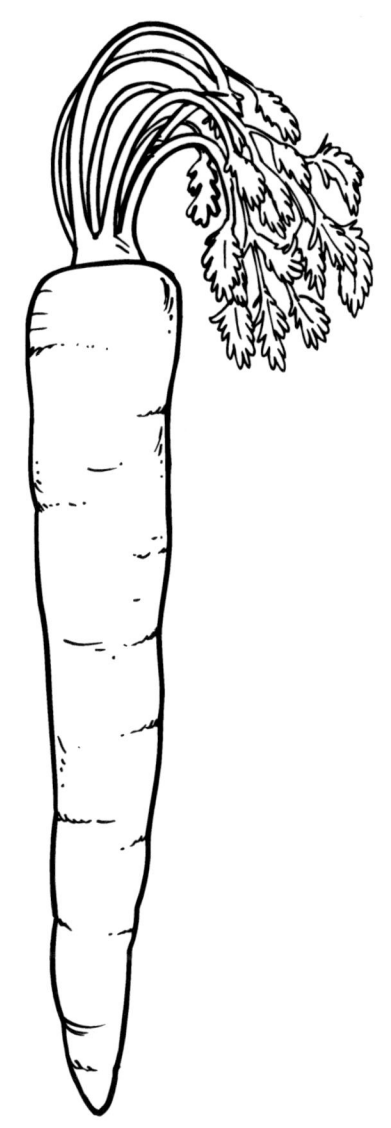

 Carrots are orange.

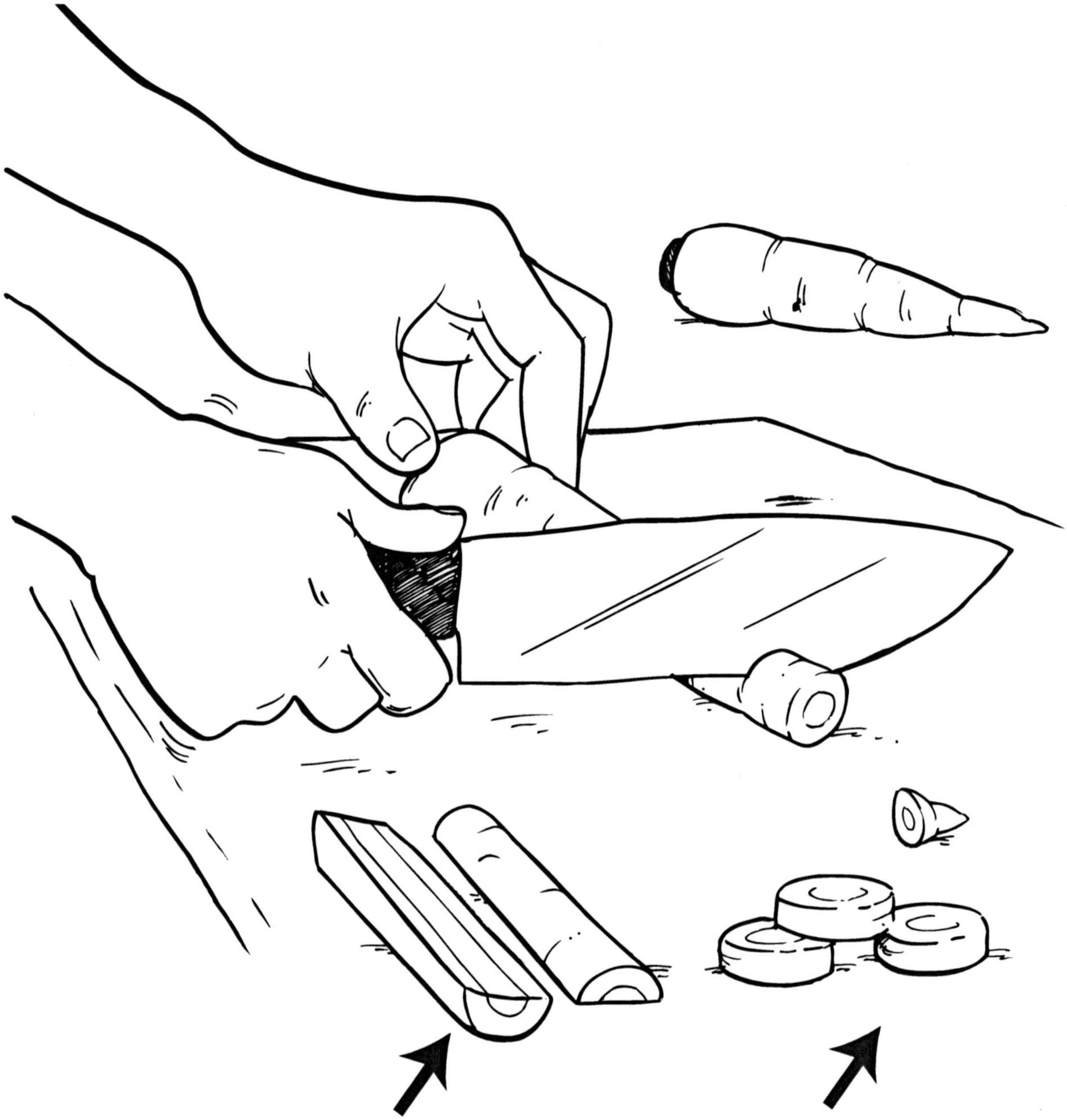

 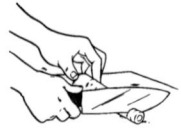  

Sometimes carrots are cut into sticks or circles.

Carrot

Sometimes carrots are cooked.

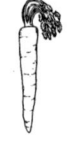  

When carrots are not cooked, they are crunchy.

Rabbits like carrots too.

Concept: Carrot

Yes-No Questions

1. Is a carrot a food?
2. Is a carrot a fruit?
3. Are carrots blue?
4. Are carrots orange?
5. Do carrots grow under the ground?
6. Do we only eat raw carrots?
7. Do we sometimes cook carrots?
8. Do we cut carrots into sticks and circles?
9. Do rabbits like carrots?
10. Do you like carrots?

Wh- and How Questions

1. What kind of food are carrots?
2. Where do carrots grow?
3. What color are carrots?
4. How do we eat cooked carrots?
5. How do we eat carrot sticks?
6. How do we make carrot circles?
7. How do carrot sticks feel?
8. Which animal likes carrots?
9. What do we do with carrots?
10. Who eats carrots?

Carrot Generalization Page

Circle the carrots. Put an X on each picture that is not a carrot.

Carrot Mini-Book

Copy this page. Cut apart the boxes on the dotted lines. Put the story in order to make a little book and staple.

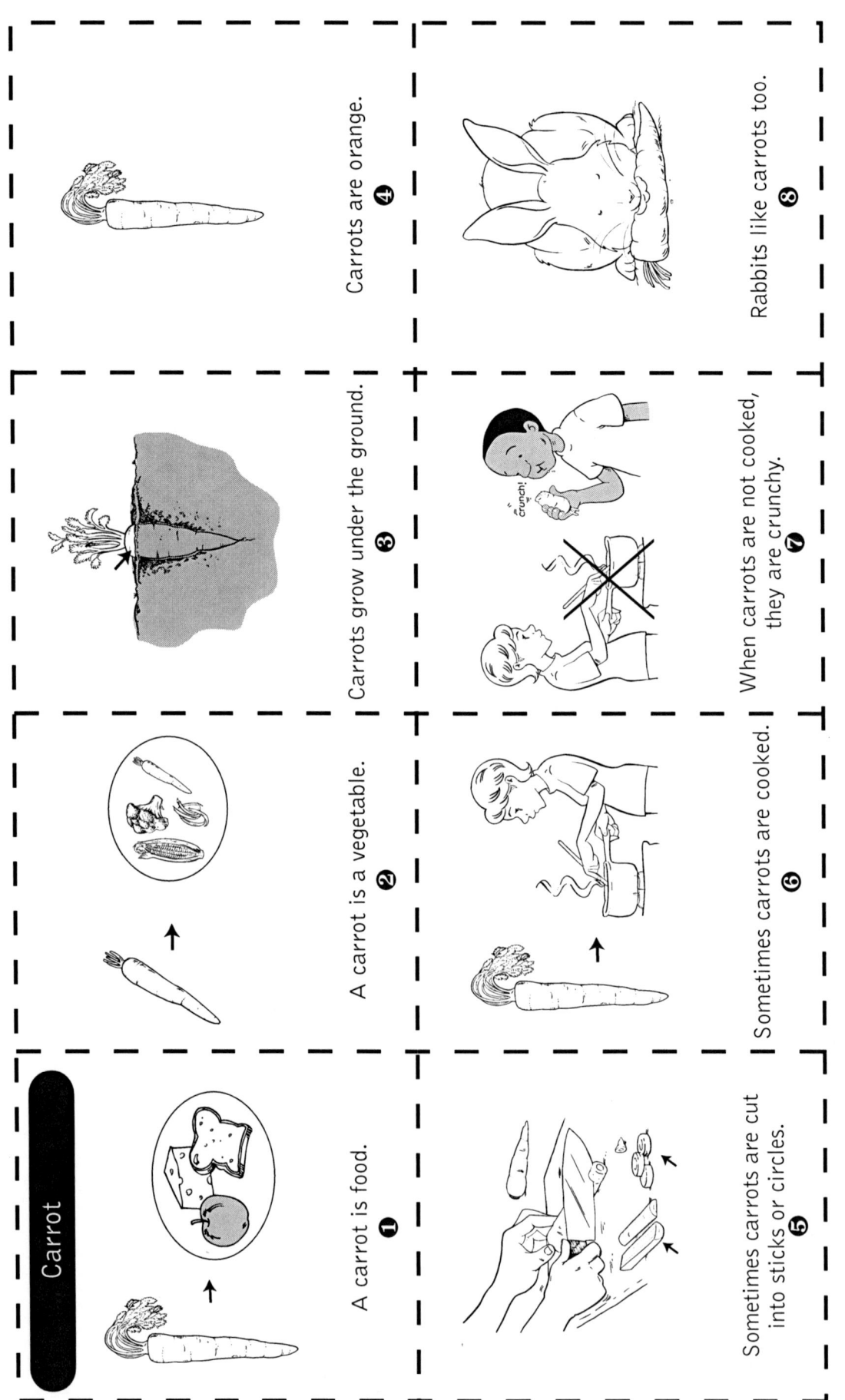

1. A carrot is food.
2. A carrot is a vegetable.
3. Carrots grow under the ground.
4. Carrots are orange.
5. Sometimes carrots are cut into sticks or circles.
6. Sometimes carrots are cooked.
7. When carrots are not cooked, they are crunchy.
8. Rabbits like carrots too.

Corn

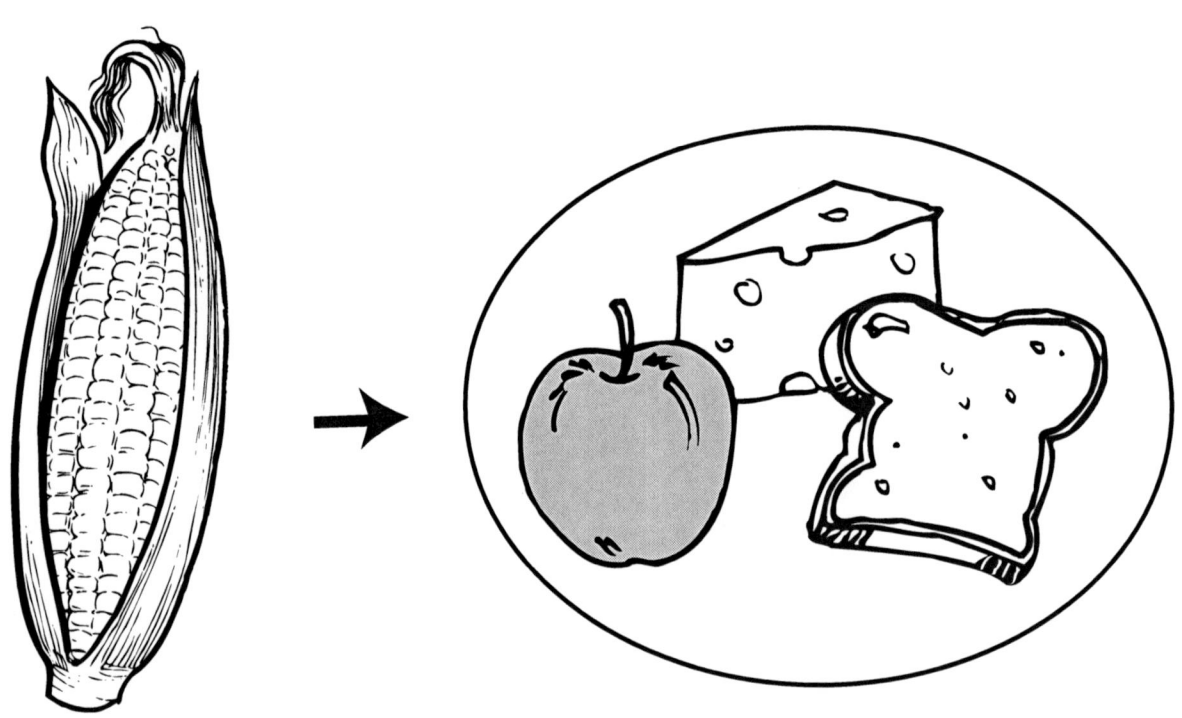

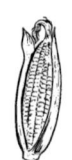 

Corn is food.

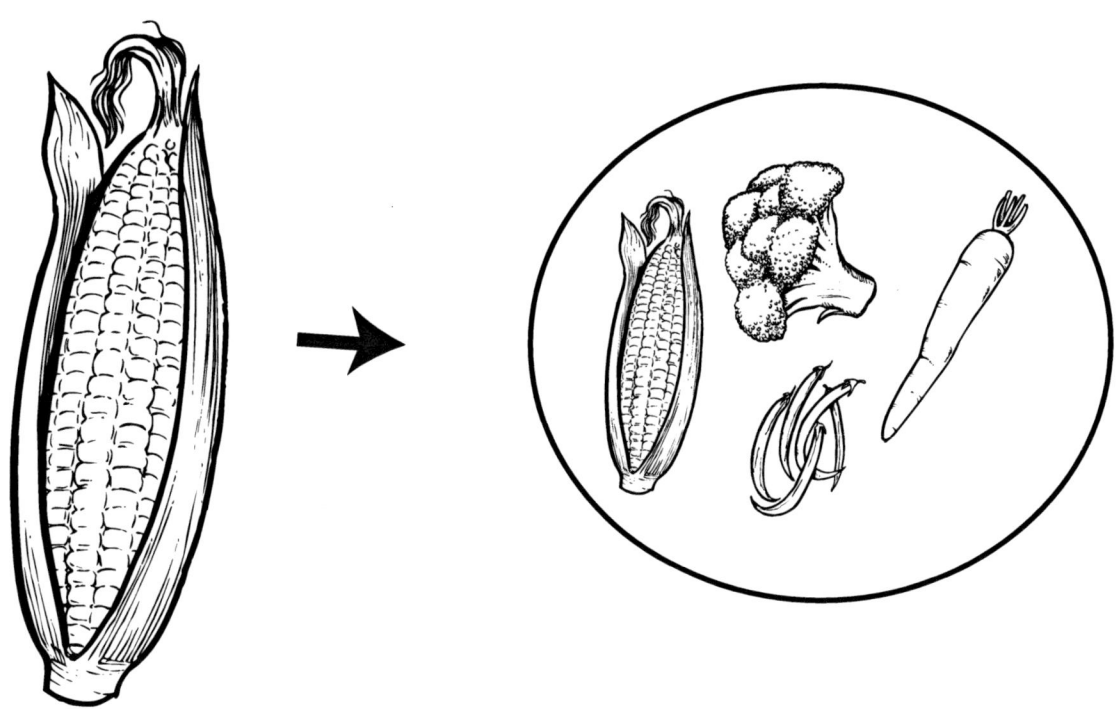

Corn is a vegetable.

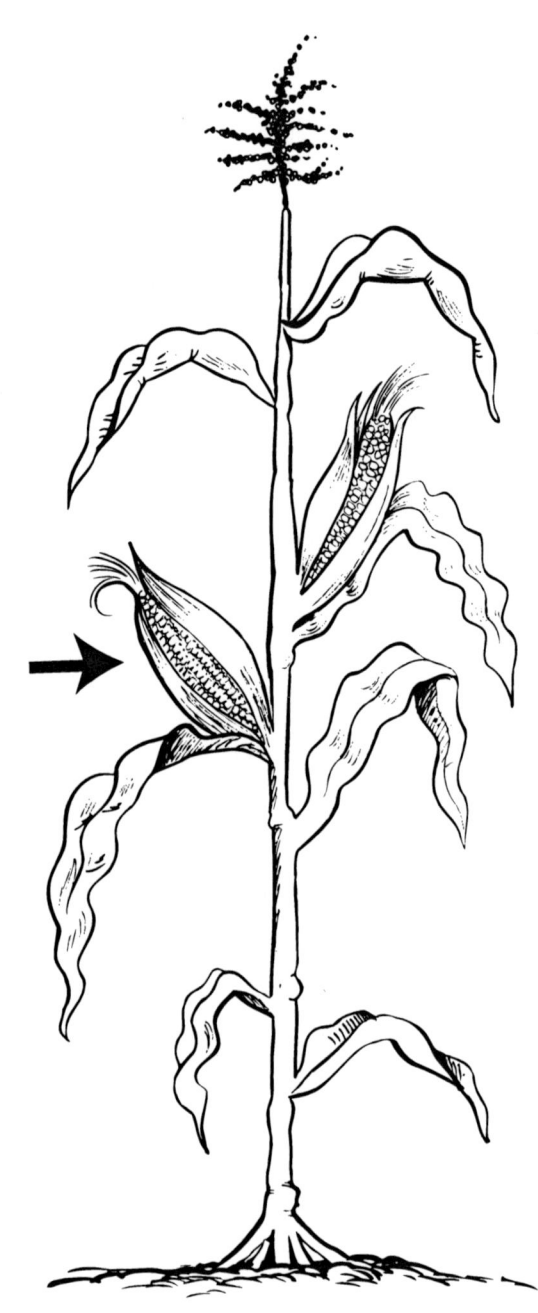

Corn grows on a stalk.

I can eat corn.

Corn is yellow.

Sometimes I eat corn with a fork.

Sometimes I eat corn on the cob with my hands.

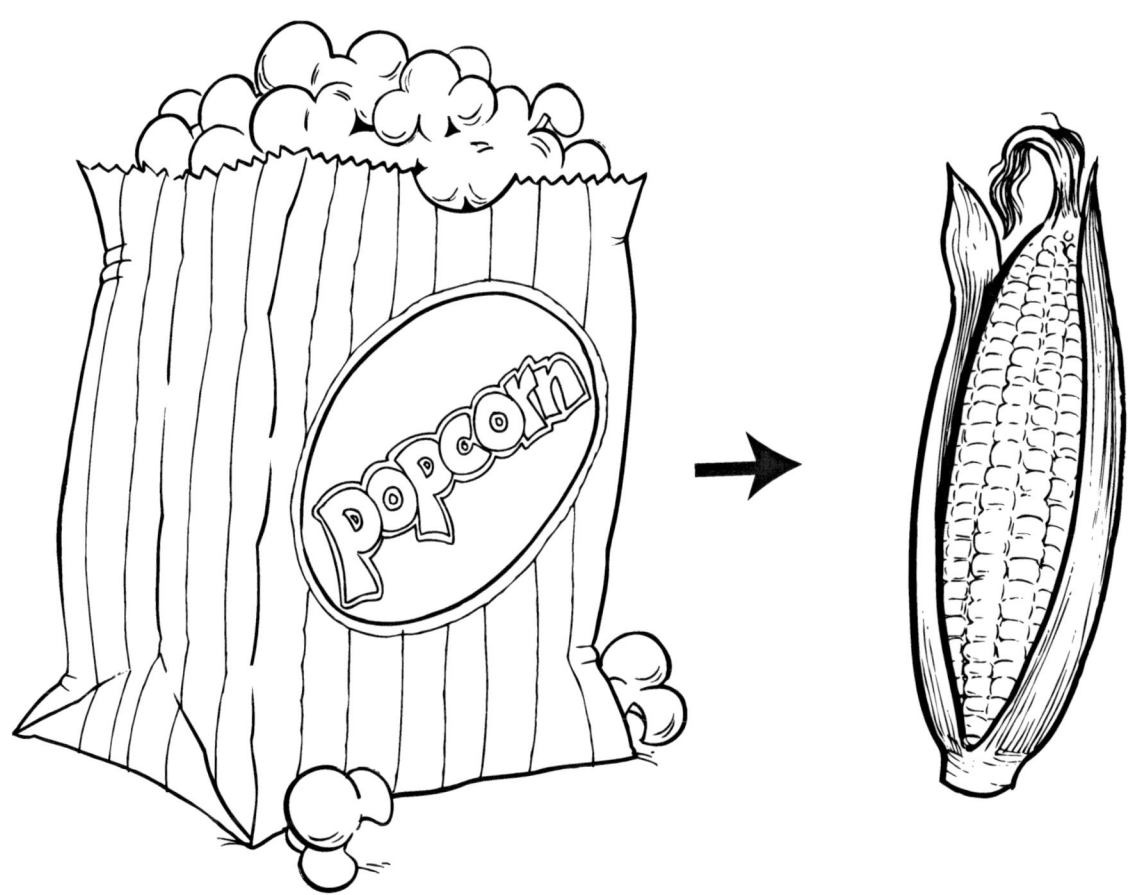

Popcorn is corn too.

Concept: Corn

Yes-No Questions

1. Do we eat corn?
2. Is corn an animal?
3. Does corn grow on trees?
4. Does corn grow on a stalk?
5. Is corn red?
6. Is corn yellow?
7. Can we eat corn with our hands?
8. Is popcorn corn?
9. Do you like corn on the cob?
10. Do you like popcorn?

Wh- and How Questions

1. Who eats corn?
2. How can you eat corn?
3. Where does corn grow?
4. What color is corn?
5. What kind of food is corn?
6. What is popcorn?
7. What color is popcorn?
8. How do you make popcorn?
9. What can you use to eat corn on the cob?
10. When do we eat corn?

Corn Generalization Page

Circle the corn. Put an X on each picture that is not corn.

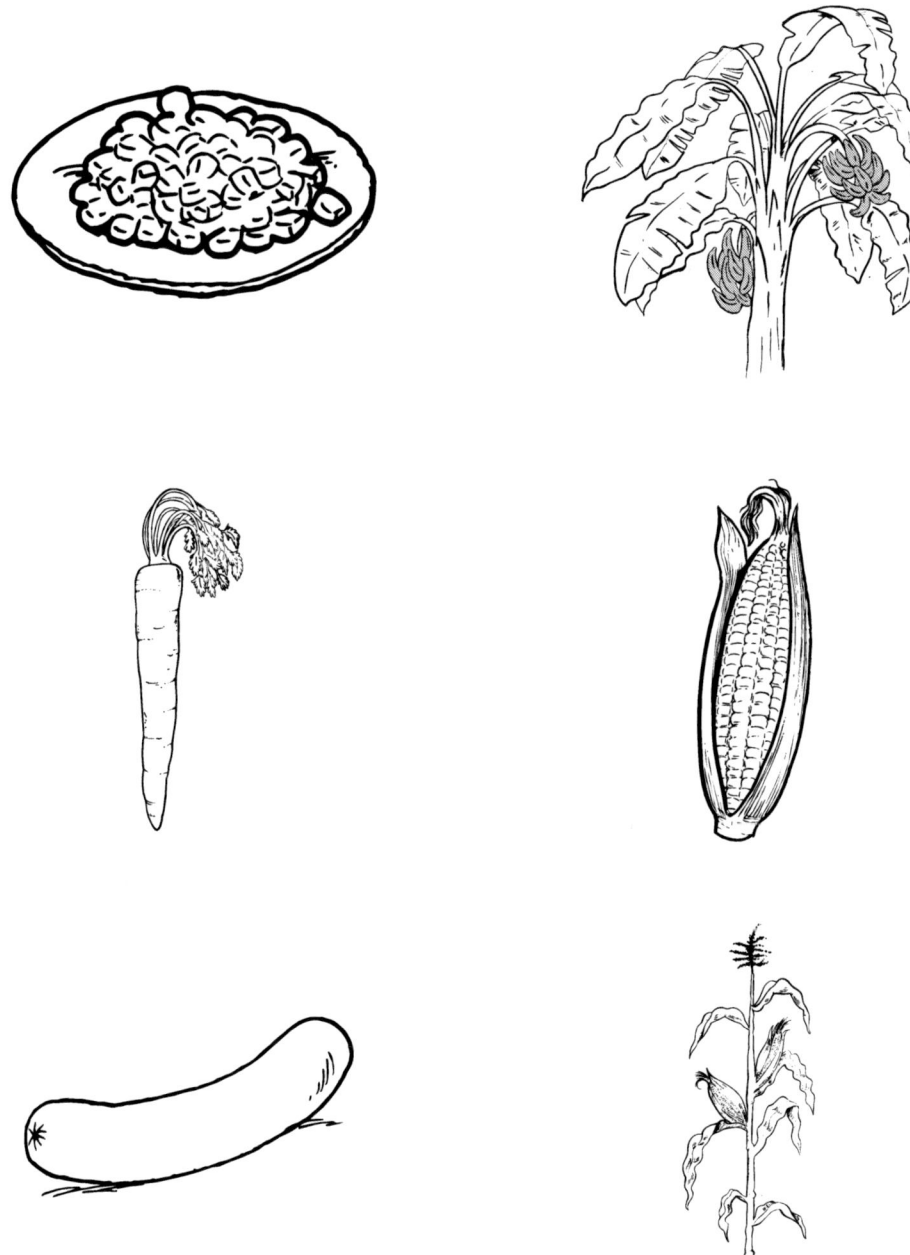

Corn Mini-Book

Copy this page. Cut apart the boxes on the dotted lines. Put the story in order to make a little book and staple.

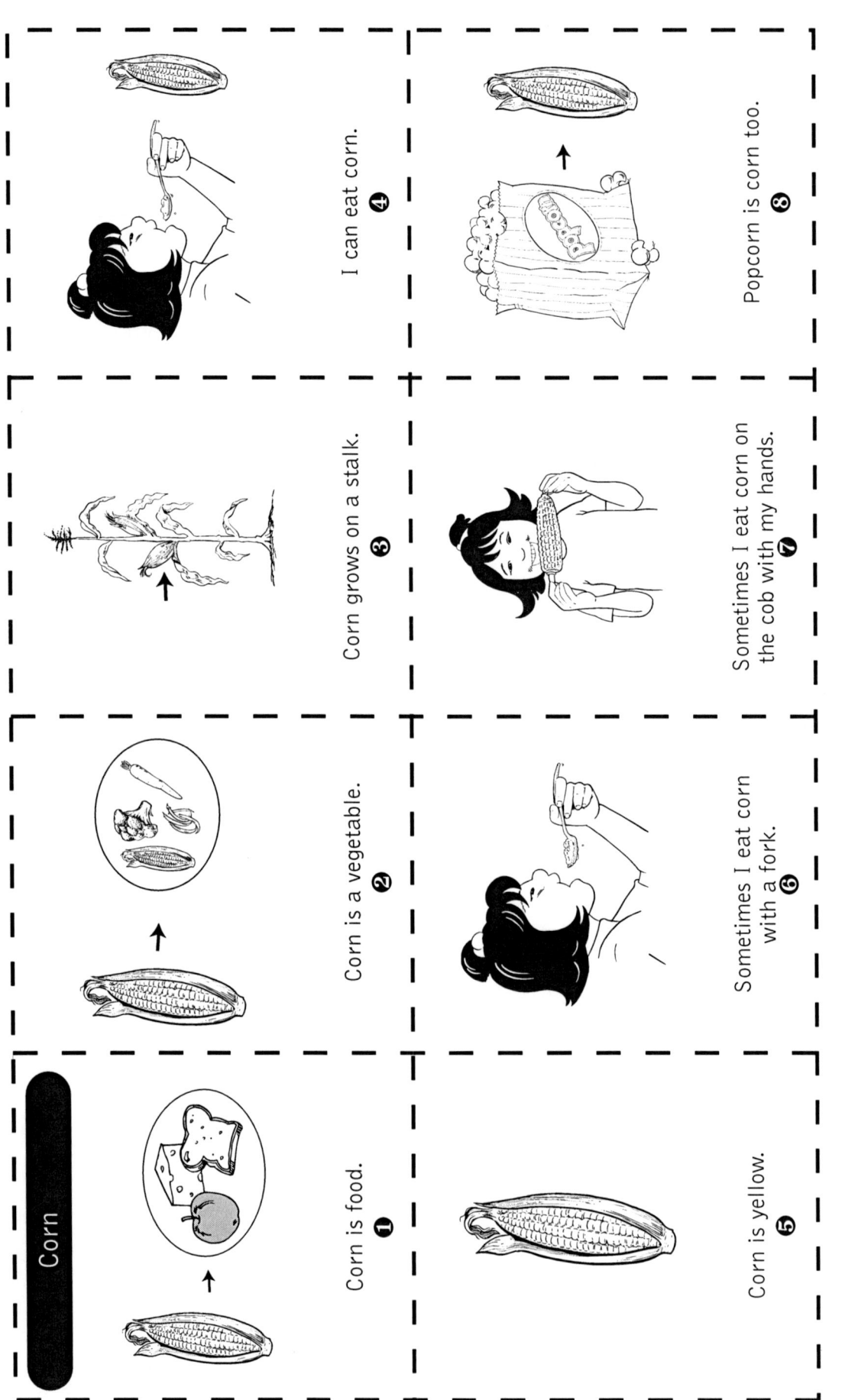

Hamburger

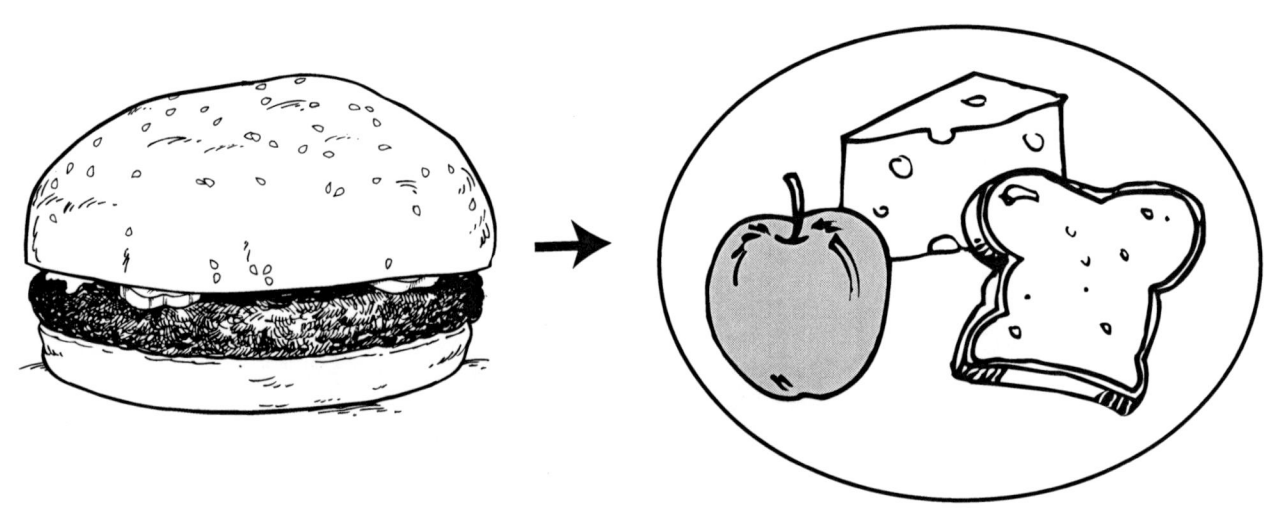

A hamburger is food.

I can eat a hamburger.

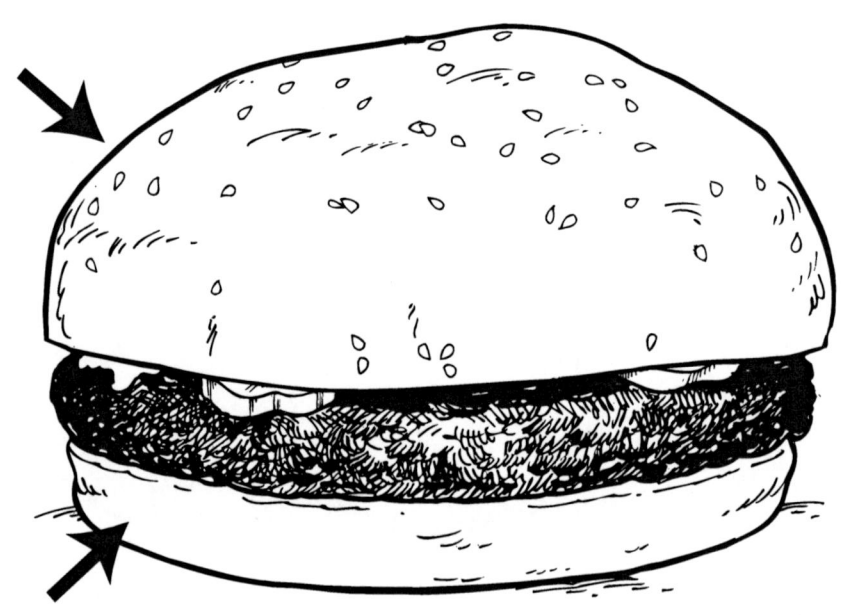

 **2**

A hamburger bun has two pieces.

A hamburger has meat in the middle.

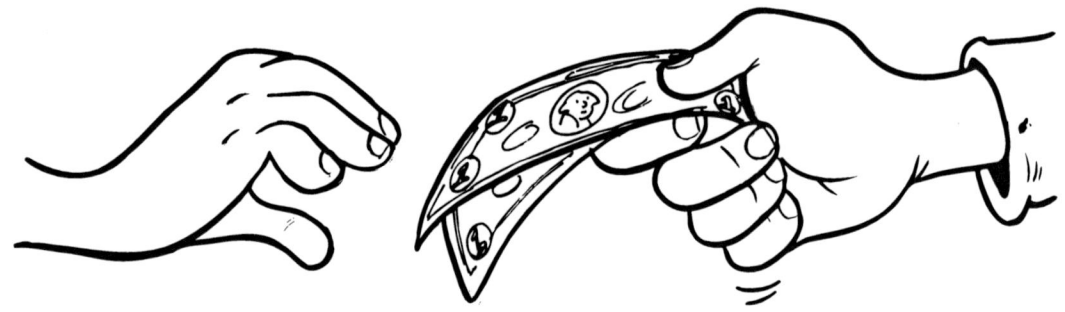

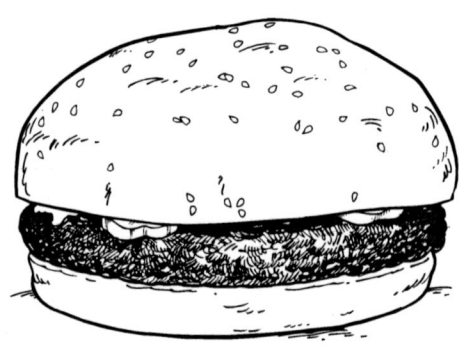

Sometimes I buy hamburgers at McDonald's or Burger King.

Sometimes people cook hamburgers on a grill.

I can put ketchup, mustard, pickles, or mayonnaise on my hamburger.

Cheese on a hamburger is called a cheeseburger.

Concept: Hamburger

Yes-No Questions

1. Is a hamburger food?
2. Does a hamburger have a bun?
3. Does a hamburger have three buns?
4. Does a hamburger have meat?
5. Is meat in the middle of a hamburger?
6. Can people cook hamburgers on a grill?
7. Do people put peanut butter on hamburgers?
8. Does a cheeseburger have cheese?
9. Can you eat a hamburger?
10. Do you like cheeseburgers?

Wh- and How Questions

1. What is a hamburger?
2. Where is the meat in a hamburger?
3. Where can you buy a hamburger?
4. Where can you cook a hamburger?
5. What can you put on a hamburger?
6. What is a cheeseburger?
7. How do you make a hamburger?
8. Why do people put ketchup on a hamburger?
9. How do you eat a hamburger?
10. Which do you like better, a hamburger or a cheeseburger?

Hamburger Generalization Page

Circle the hamburgers. Put an X on each picture that is not a hamburger.

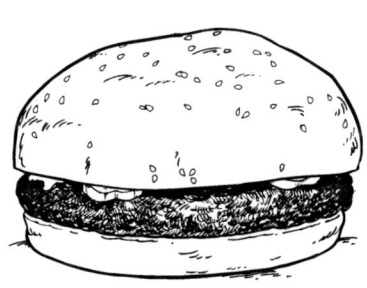

Hamburger Mini-Book

Copy this page. Cut apart the boxes on the dotted lines. Put the story in order to make a little book and staple.

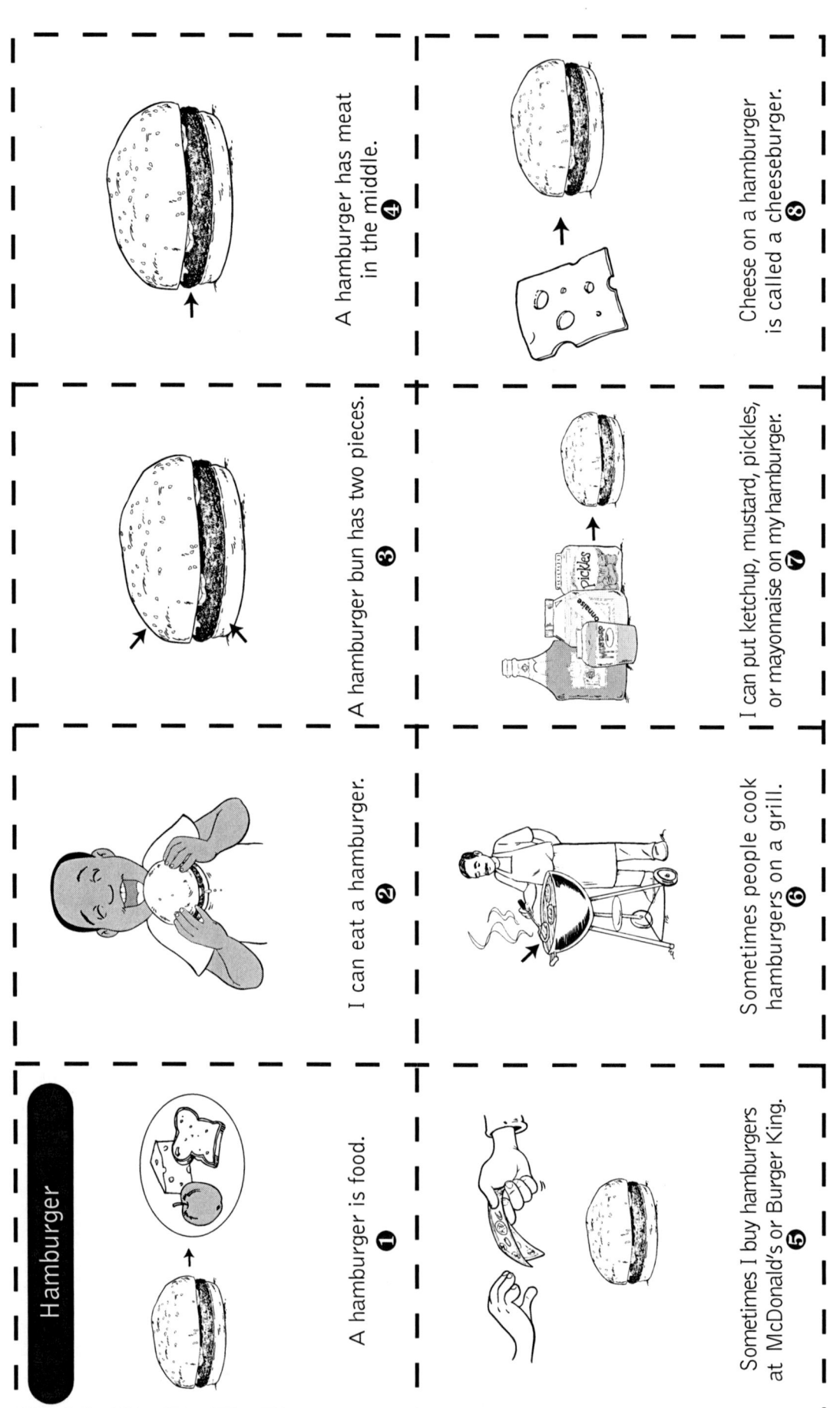

Hamburger

A hamburger is food. ❶

I can eat a hamburger. ❷

A hamburger bun has two pieces. ❸

A hamburger has meat in the middle. ❹

Sometimes I buy hamburgers at McDonald's or Burger King. ❺

Sometimes people cook hamburgers on a grill. ❻

I can put ketchup, mustard, pickles, or mayonnaise on my hamburger. ❼

Cheese on a hamburger is called a cheeseburger. ❽

Hamburger
Concept Development

116

Copyright © 2001 LinguiSystems, Inc.

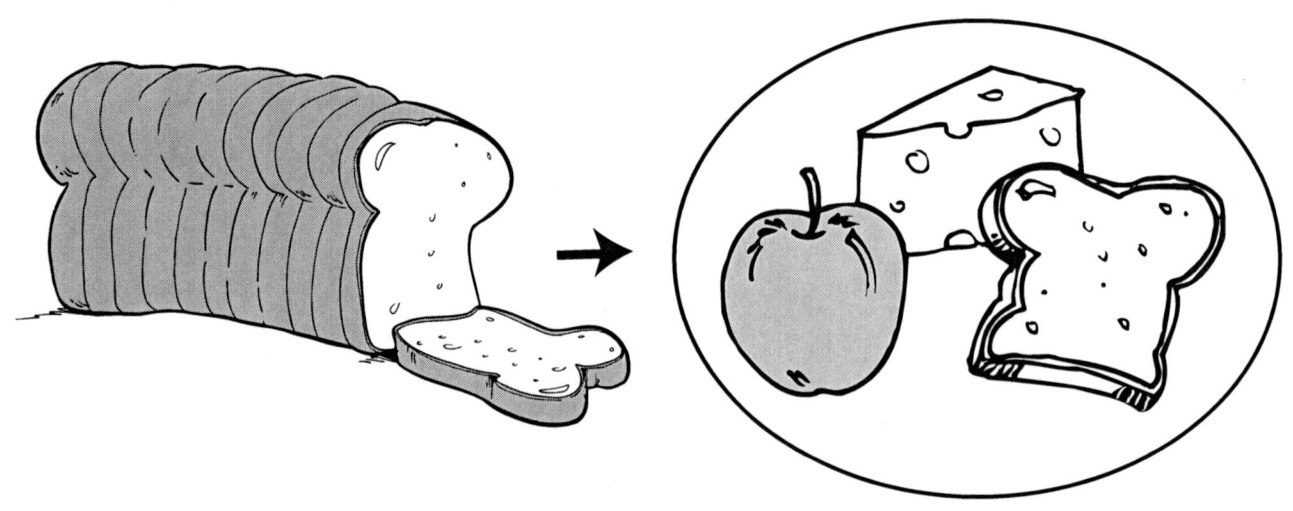

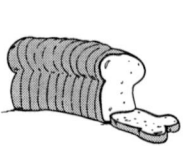 

Bread is food.

I can eat bread.

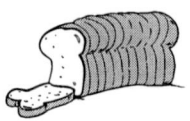

Bread comes in a loaf.

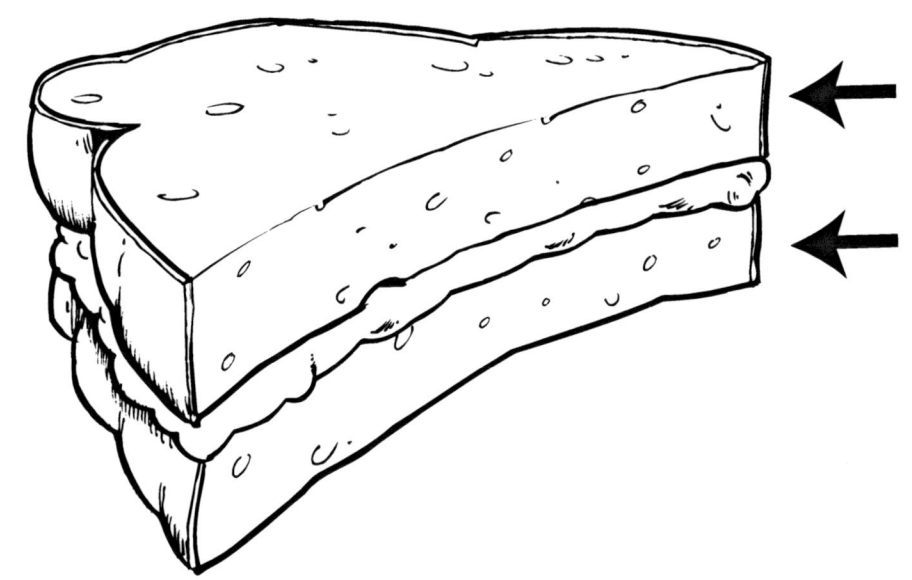

I can make a sandwich with bread.

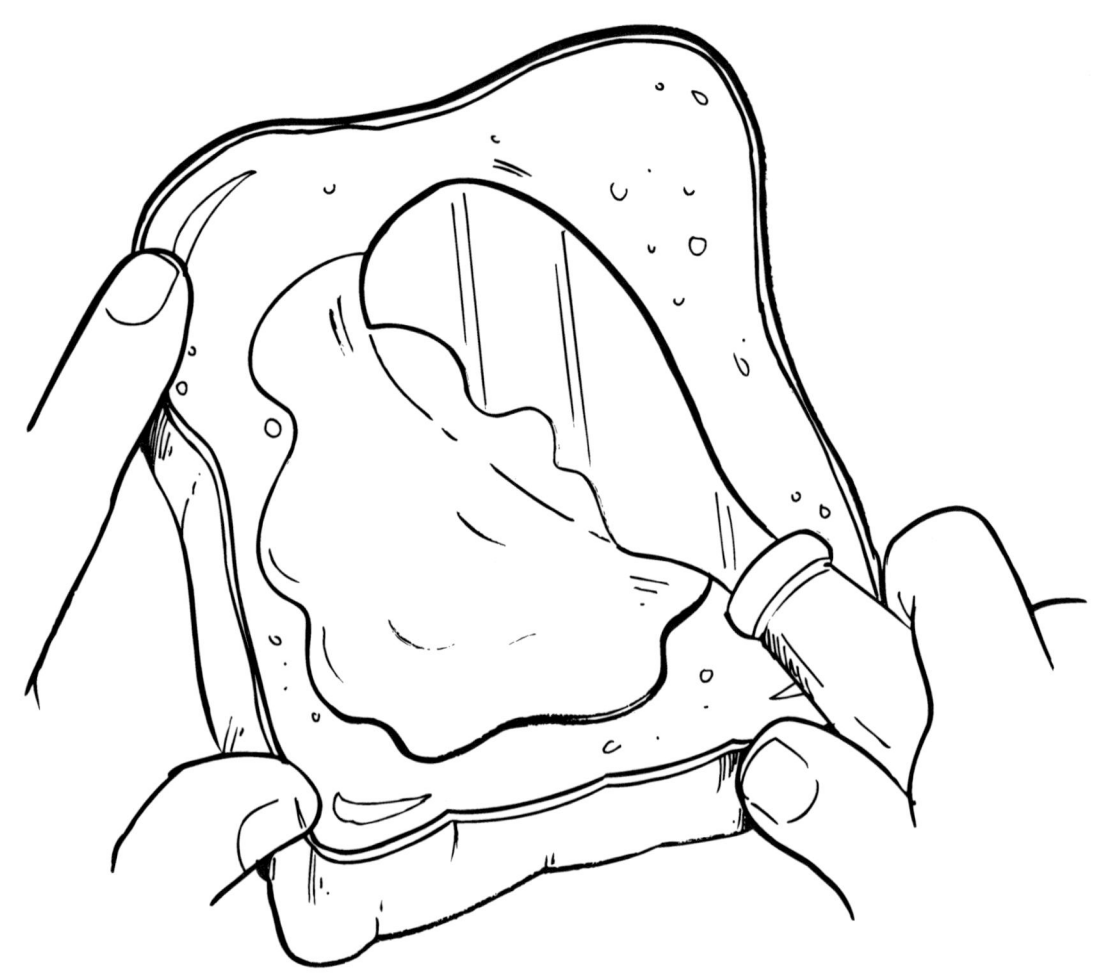

  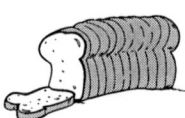

I can put butter on bread.

I can toast bread.

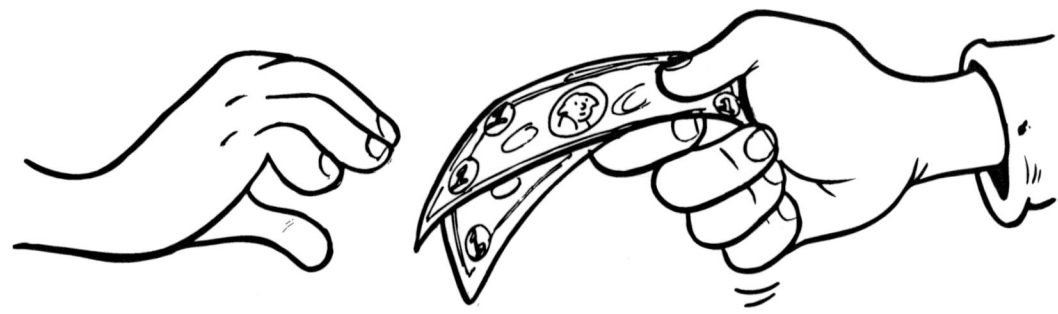

We buy bread at a store.

 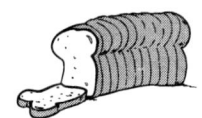 

Sometimes we bake bread at home.

Concept: Bread

Yes-No Questions

1. Is bread a food?
2. Do you eat bread?
3. Does bread come in a loaf?
4. Do you put grass on bread?
5. Do people put butter on bread?
6. Can we toast bread?
7. Are sandwiches made with bread?
8. Do people make bread on a grill?
9. Do people bake bread in an oven?
10. Do you like bread?

Wh- and How Questions

1. What is bread?
2. Who eats bread?
3. What is a loaf?
4. Where can you put butter?
5. How do you make toast?
6. Where can you buy bread?
7. Where can you bake bread at home?
8. How do you make a sandwich?
9. When do we eat bread?
10. Which do you like better, bread or toast?

Bread Generalization Page

Circle the bread. Put an X on each picture that is not bread.

Bread Mini-Book

Copy this page. Cut apart the boxes on the dotted lines. Put the story in order to make a little book and staple.

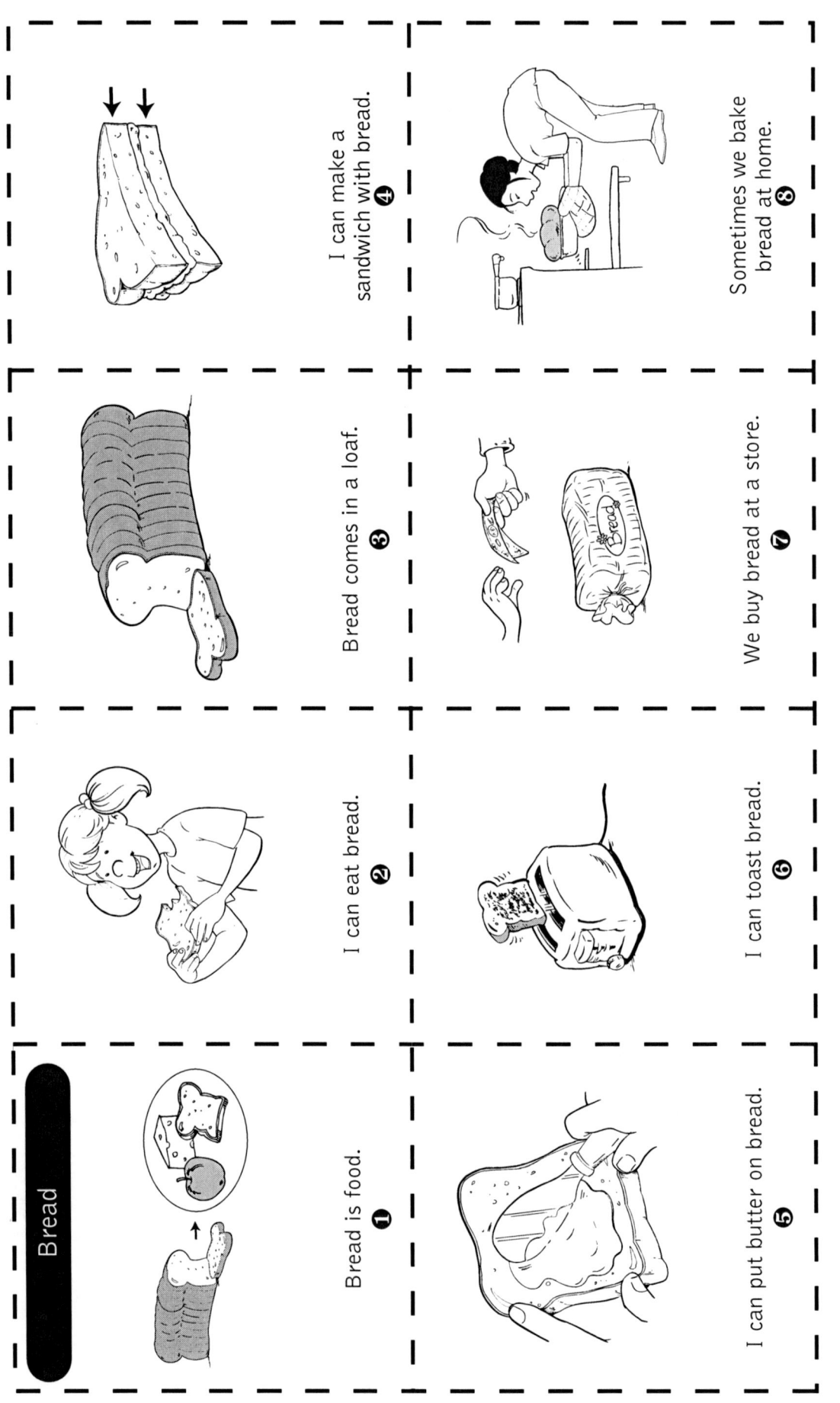

Water Activity: Make Ice

Materials: ice trays, small pitcher, water, timer, freezer

Have the child fill an ice tray with water from the pitcher. Open the freezer and let the child feel the cold air and touch the cold insides. Place the tray in the freezer and set the timer. When the timer goes off, let the child check the ice tray. Give the child an ice cube to taste and feel. You might also want to mix the water with a powdered fruit drink before making ice cubes.

Water Activity: Float Boats

Materials: photographs of a variety of boats; variety of toy boats; small plastic tub, water table, or wading pool

Show the child pictures of the different boats. Label each picture as a boat. Fill the container with water. Give the child one of the toy boats. Have the child float the boat in the water. Encourage the child to blow the boat to move it across the water. You can also give the child other water toys such as funnels, pitchers, and cups for the child to splash and play with.

Milk Activity: Make Butter

Materials: a pint of whipping cream, baby food jars or other jars with tight-fitting lids, crackers or small pieces of bread, plastic knife

Pour some cream (1/3 –1/2 full) into a baby food jar. The amount of cream depends on the size of the jar. Make sure the lid is on tight. Prompt the child to "shake, shake, shake." Butter will form in about 10-15 minutes. Open the jar and pour off any liquid so that only the butter remains. Spread the butter on crackers or small pieces of bread.

Sandwich Activity: Make a Sandwich

Materials: sandwich bread, peanut butter, jelly, plastic knife, plate

Help the child make a peanut butter and jelly sandwich.

Ice Cream Activity: Make Ice Cream

Note: This recipe will make one child's serving.

Materials: ½ c. milk, 1 T. sugar, ¼ tsp. vanilla, mixing bowl, 2-3 cups crushed ice, 6 T. rock salt, sandwich-size zippered plastic bag, gallon-size zippered plastic bag, plastic spoon

Mix the milk, sugar, and vanilla flavoring in the bowl. Pour into the sandwich bag and seal. Put the ice, salt, and sandwich bag into the gallon-size bag and seal. Have the child shake and twist the bag. In two to five minutes, the milk mixture will be slushy ice cream. Give the child the little bag and a plastic spoon so he can enjoy the ice cream.

Apple Activity: Make Applesauce

Materials: 3 large apples, ½ - ¾ cup apple juice, ½ tsp. cinnamon, apple peeler, sharp knife, small saucepan, stove, spoons, bowls

Peel the apples and cut into small pieces. Place apple pieces in saucepan or electric skillet. Add apple juice and cinnamon. Cook apples uncovered over medium heat. Cook until apples are soft (about 15 minutes). Mash and eat.

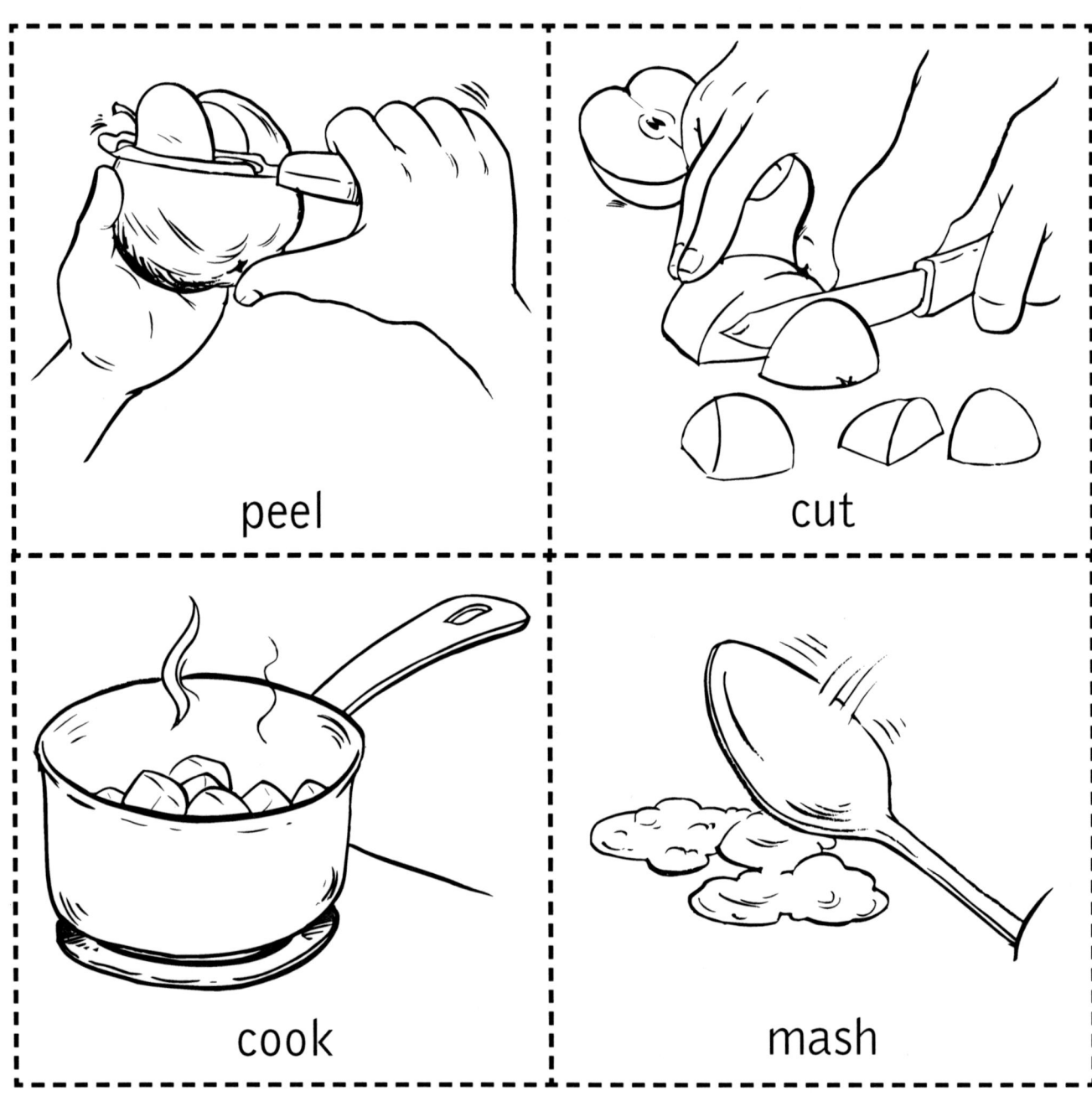

Apple Activity: Apple Sort

Materials: red, green, and yellow apples; 3 containers, knife

Have the child sort the apples by color into the containers. Then cut the apples. Encourage the child to taste and compare the apples.

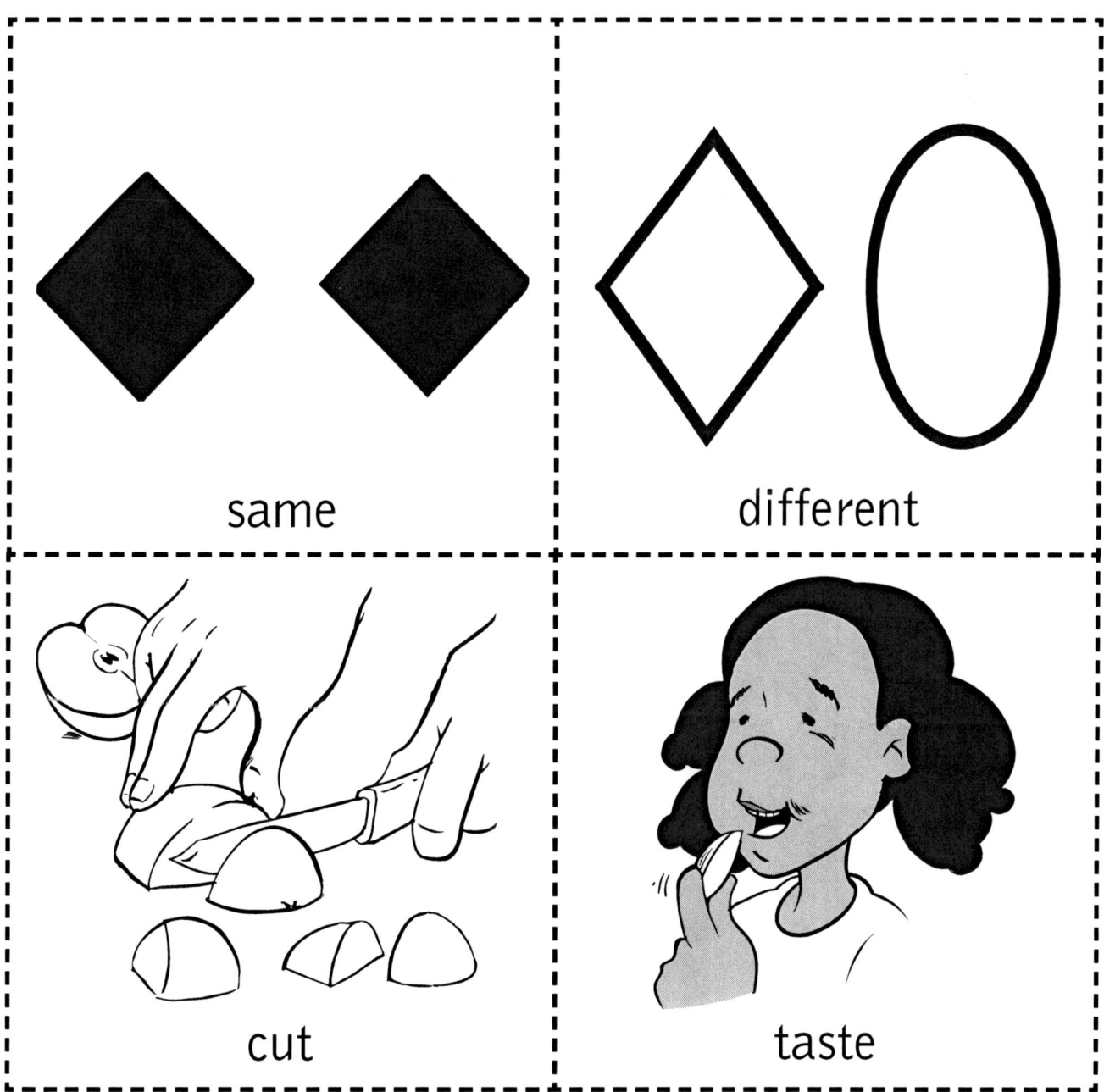

Banana Activity: Banana Tasting

Materials: several bananas, plastic knife, plate

Give the child a banana. If necessary, help the child peel the banana. Eat the banana as is or cut the banana with the knife into small pieces before eating.

Carrot Activity: Carrot Tasting

Materials: carrots, potato peeler, sharp knife, stove, small saucepan, plates

Peel the carrots and then divide them into three groups. Leave some carrots whole, cut some carrots into sticks and circles, cut the third group into circles and cook over low heat. When the carrots are finished cooking, encourage the child to taste a carrot from all three groups.

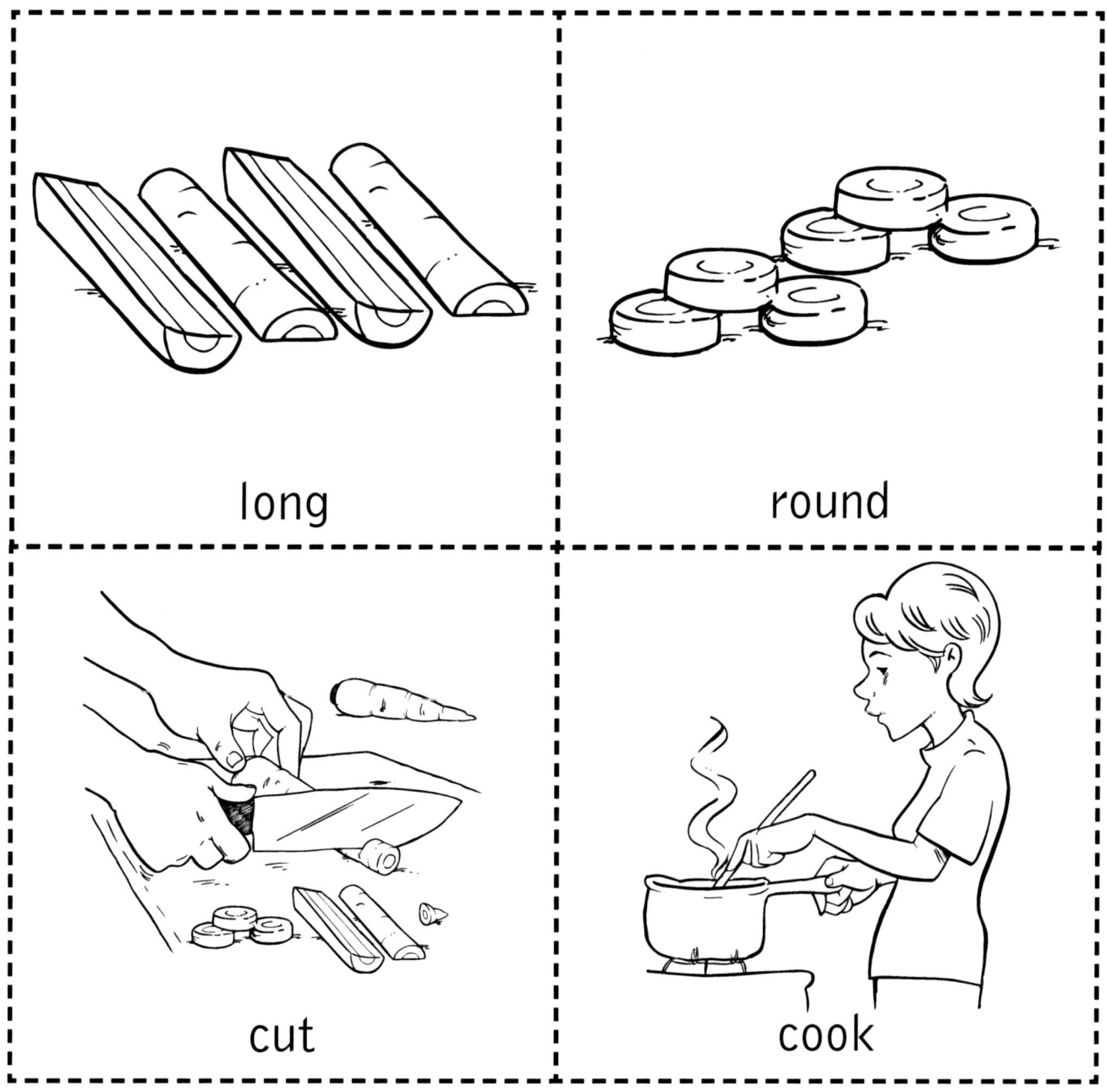

Concept Development

Carrot Activity: Grow Carrots

Materials: carrot seeds, paper cups, potting soil, water

Fill a cup with potting soil. Plant a few carrot seeds in the soil. Cover the seeds with dirt. Water and place the cup in a sunny window. As the carrots begin to sprout (10-18 days), talk about growing using the Picture Prompt Card. Remind the child to water the plant periodically. After three to four weeks, a small carrot should be formed. Pull it and show it to the child. Wash it, peel it, and eat it.

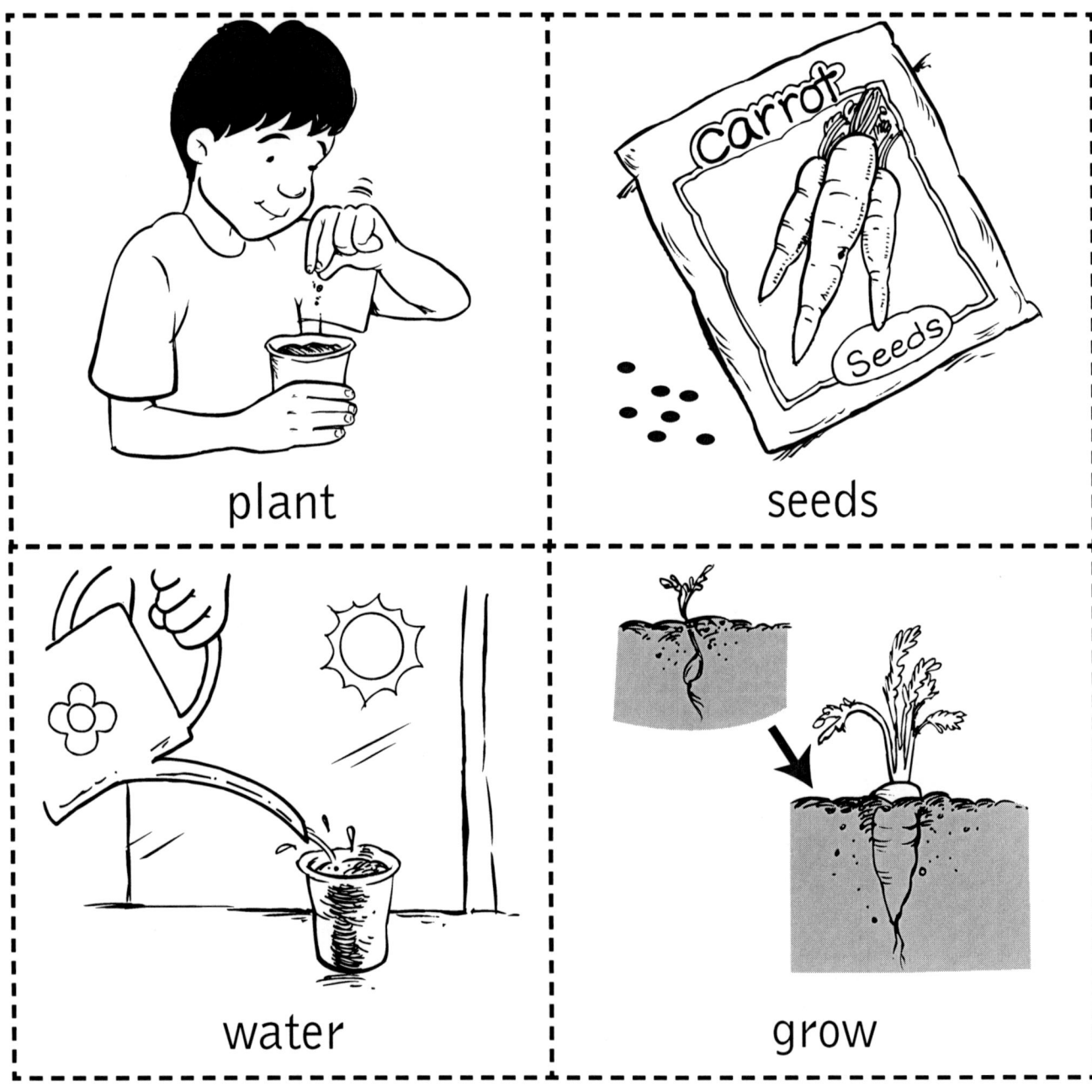

Corn Activity: Pop Popcorn*

Materials: ½ c. popcorn kernels, 1 T. vegetable oil, pot with lid, stove

Make popcorn the old-fashioned way! Show the child the popcorn kernels. Preheat the pan. Add the oil and popcorn to the pan and cover. Cook popcorn over high heat while shaking the pan constantly. After about one minute, you will hear the popcorn popping. When the popcorn stops popping, turn off the stove and remove the pan from the heat. Be careful when taking off the lid. Eat and enjoy!

*Popcorn can cause choking. Be careful when small children are eating the popcorn.

Corn Activity: Corn Tasting

Materials: ears of corn, large pot, small pot with lid, sharp knife, water, butter, salt, plates, plastic knives and forks

Husk the corn. Divide the corn into two groups. Fill the large pot half full of water. Bring the water to a rapid boil. Place the ears from the first group of corn into the large pot. Boil the corn for 3-5 minutes until tender. Slice the kernels off the ears in the other group. Simmer the corn kernels in their own juice in the small pot, covered, until tender (several minutes). When the ears of corn and the corn kernels are cooked, let the child taste them. Serve with butter and salt.

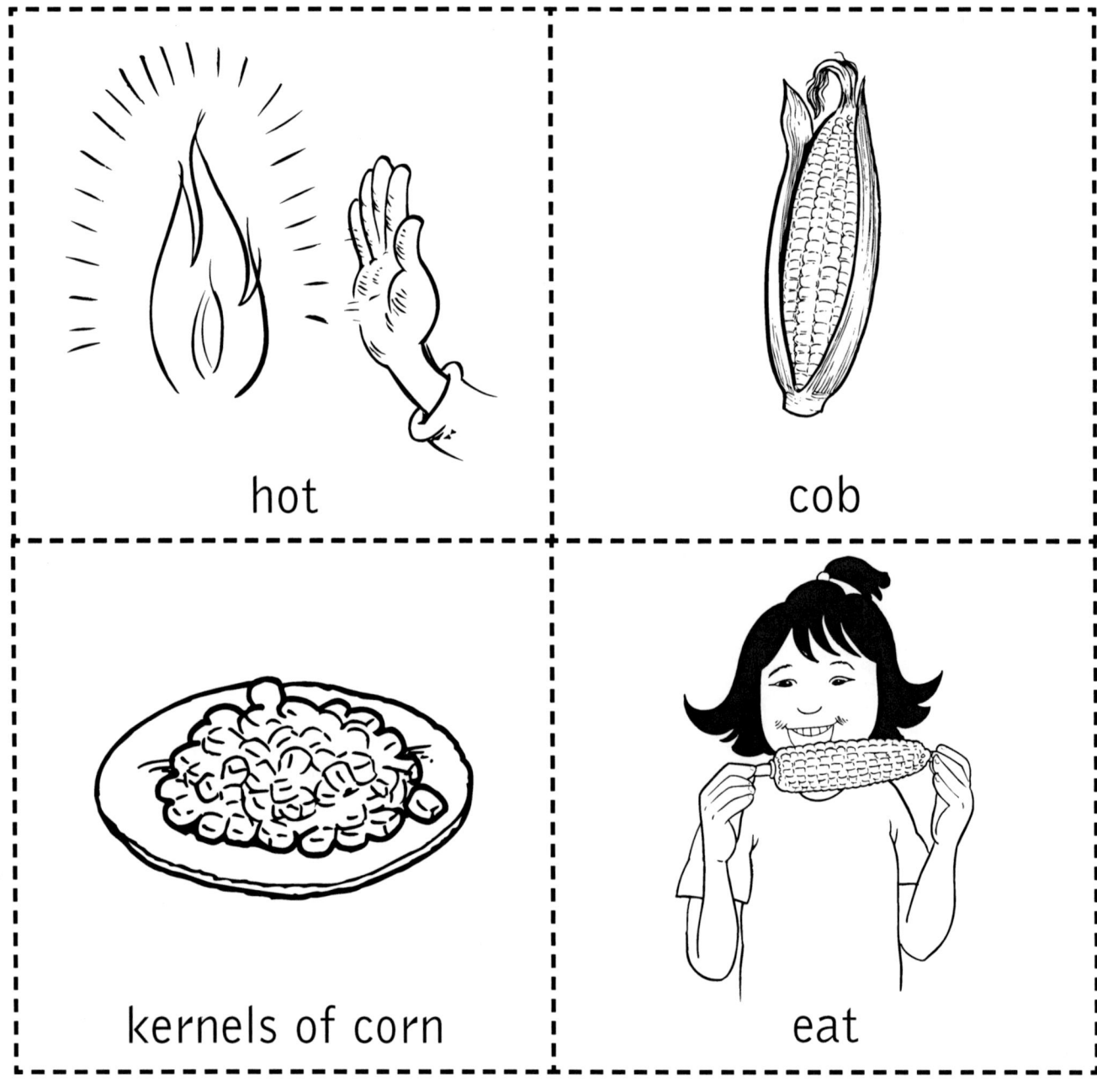

Hamburger Activity: Make Hamburgers

Materials: 1 lb. ground beef, hamburger buns, salt, pepper, variety of condiments (mayonnaise, ketchup, etc.), skillet, stove, spatula, plates, plastic knives

Help the child shape a hamburger patty. Have the child wash his hands well when done. Season with salt and pepper if desired. Cook hamburger patty, uncovered, over medium heat until the juices run clear. Turn hamburgers over halfway through cooking time. (If beef is very lean, you may need to add a little oil to the pan.) Remove patty from the heat. Allow the child to spread condiments of choice on his hamburger bun.

Bread Activity: Make Toast

Materials: toaster, bread, butter, plastic knife

Let the child put the bread into the toaster and push down the handle. When it pops up, use the knife to spread the butter. Encourage the child to eat the toast.

bread

toast (push down)

pop up

toast

Suggested Literature

Food
We Like Fruit by Millen Lee
Fruit: A First Discovery Book by Gallimard Jeunesse & Pascal de Bourgoing
Good to Eat by Rebel Williams
Eating the Alphabet by Lois Ehlert

Water
Where is Water? by Kelly Paulsen
I am Water by Jean Marzollo

Milk
Milk From Cow to Carton by Aliki

Sandwich
How to Make a Sandwich by Claudette C. Mitchell, Grace R. Porter, & Patricia Cousin

Apple
Apples and Pumpkins by Anne Rockwell

Bread
Bread, Bread, Bread by Anne Morris
Everybody Eats Bread by Diana Noonan